"Stories to teach you how to live happily and safely in the digital world"
Bo Eason – Seven Time National Bestselling Author

Happily Ever Cyber!™

How To Protect Yourself Against Hackers, Scammers, and Cybermonsters™

By
Sandra Estok
Foreword by Dave Tyson

This book is dedicated to what makes
our dreams come true.

Contents

Endorsements

Sandra Estok's book *"Happily Ever Cyber!"* is a compelling review and an educational tool for anyone's needs. Sandra's commentary and excerpts are exceptionally beneficial as she speaks to the reality of the cyber landscape through her extensive years of expertise in the privacy and security profession. Readers will be anxious to put her suggestions and guidance into their everyday lives. As a cybersecurity industry professional of 33 years, I found this book to be engaging, interactive and a go to reference for all ages.

Pamela Fusco

Proud US Navy Veteran

From the start, author Sandra Estok's *Happily Ever Cyber!* quickly provides simple and easy-to-understand connections and concepts to simplify and make sense of our evolving technology world, using concepts we find in our world all around us.

This book takes you from being confused about our "digital world" to understanding cyber and how to best protect yourself from the ever-increasing cyber risks that can impact you. Sandra Estok has enabled readers to not be a victim, but to discover they can be in control of protecting their digital world. This book should "simply" be a requirement for everyone using technology.

Jeff Spivey, CRISC, CPP, PSP

CEO Security Risk Management Inc

Prior Int'l Board ISACA - Prior Int'l President
ASIS International

This book will transform the way you perceive cybersecurity! Sandra moves away from technical instructions and instead connects her personal life stories to easily understandable ways to protect our information. A must read!

Sandra Yancey

CEO and Founder eWomenNetwork, Inc.

CNN American Hero

In her new book, *Happily Ever Cyber!* Sandra Estok uses first-hand stories to teach you how to live happily and safely in the digital world.

Bo Eason

Athlete, Speaker, Performer, Playwright and 7-Time National Best-Selling Author of There's No Plan B for Your A-Game

Happily Ever Cyber! is insightful, easy and fun to read. Sandra Estok gives you a simple understanding of the world of cybercrime and identity theft, and why protecting ourselves is so important in our world today. Bottom line — this book ROCKS!

Craig Duswalt, Keynote Speaker, Author, Podcaster

Creator of the brands RockStar Marketing and Rock Your Life

A perfect primer for those looking to learn about the complex and scary world of cybersecurity. This book uses engaging personal stories and provides great examples of how to protect ourselves from becoming a cybercrime victim.

Bozena Kalita
Chief Digital Officer at PenFed Credit Union

It is not easy to find an expert who puts themselves in your place, to present these topics in a simple, practical, and easily understandable way. Sandra Estok guides you in creating safe habits with which to navigate the cybersecurity ecosystem, helps you develop that sense that will allow you to detect when you may be at risk, as well as explain what you should do in advance to avoid getting hurt.

Happily Ever Cyber! presents the principles that allow us to protect what matters most: our personal security and the safety of our loved ones.

As you read this book, you will find a friend who is willing to hold your hand and immerse with you in the complex but necessary cyber-world.

David Flores
Nielsen Executive

Sandra Estok has taken the mystery out of cybersecurity and the jargon surrounding it.

Happily Ever Cyber! the first book in the series helps us to better understand what it is and how to defend ourselves against cybercrime. The book is done in a very informative and entertaining manner. I can't wait for the next book in the series.

R.W. Bowman
Director of Global Computer Engineering (Retired)

In *Happily Ever Cyber!*, Sandra takes on the complex, ever-evolving world of cybersecurity and provides understandable insights and practical methods you can use today to help protect yourself. Whether you are technology savvy or just someone who wants to feel safe using your phone or computer, this quick, engaging read has something for everyone.

Paula Powell

Senior Director IT (Retired)

I have been in IT-related fields for about 40 years and one of the biggest challenges I faced was helping the audience understand cybersecurity. It is the first time I have seen the mystery of cybersecurity deciphered in such rich, yet simple terms.

The author breaks down cybersecurity using very simple personal stories, sometimes very hilarious, that illustrate situations that could happen to anyone. The author helps us identify our fears, understand the unknown, and guides us to own the resolution through our actions.

This is a must-read book for you to face the cyber world.

Alejandro J. Briceno

IT Director, S.C. Johnson and Son Inc. (Retired)

Topics like technology and cybersecurity often hide behind a veil of complexity making them difficult or even undesirable to spend the necessary time required to understand them. As more of our daily lives continue to become digitized online the importance of understanding cybersecurity common practices also increases. Sandra's non-technical approach to explaining these topics and associating them with her personal life stories helps make these complex concepts easily approachable by everyone at every level. Don't be the low-hanging fruit!

Mark Ward
SVP Chief Information Security Officer
Johnson Bank

This book is a riveting read and what makes it so unique is that the author has chosen challenges and experiences from her past and made it relatable to the cybersecurity topics.

James Lim
Managing Consultant
Integrity Risk Solutions

Sandra always brings dedication and focus to the work she does. The tools and ideas presented in *Happily Ever Cyber!* have been developed through diligent research, practical application, adaptation and refinement as the ever-changing world of cybersecurity continues to spin. Take heed - you'll be glad you did!

Jeffrey Bornman
Trainer and Coach

This book is outstanding! For anyone one who wants a quick, highly-focused understanding of what is important and what you need to do relative to cybersecurity, this is the book. It is a series of study guides for cybersecurity knowledge and interpretation. It includes great best practices and recommendations on next steps to start your cybersecurity journey and program. A must have addition to your cybersecurity reference library.

C. Steve Langer, Vice President of Information Technology (Head of Global IT)

Modine Manufacturing Company

This book keeps readers' attention by intermixing Sandra's personal and professional stories, as well as pertinent information regarding cybersecurity.

I specifically appreciated the nuts and bolts of the cybersecurity issues and the definition of terms, as I am not a technical person. The reflection areas at the end of each chapter helped me gain awareness and retain the information I was unfamiliar with.

Happily Ever Cyber! provides thought-provoking information and examples for the everyday person. It's a good resource to understand cybersecurity.

Amy Roufus

Cybersecurity can be overwhelming. The constant war against cybercriminals is never-ending. Sandra associates cybersecurity circumstances with real life non-cyber anecdotes that help you visualize these risks from a more human perspective.

Even as I lead a network security team for businesses, it helped me internalize the vulnerabilities I personally faced, and to understand what actions to take – the tailor's wife is the worst clad! I can't wait to read the upcoming books in the series!

Camilo Cuartas

Manager B2B Technology

Connectivity and Security Product Engineering Liberty Latin America

Foreword

After 30 years in the security industry, I have learned a few essential truths, of which two really stand out: The first is *nothing is free on the Internet*, and the second is *people are not as skeptical on the Internet as they are in real life*, and this can get them into trouble.

Most people would not walk down a dark alley to buy a watch from the trunk of a car from a "scary looking guy;" but they will click on any link in an email and believe whatever is sent to them by people they have never met. This leads me to believe that most people are just unaware of the risks because of the ease of use and lack of immediate threat.

As the Chief Information Security Officer, the role primarily charged with protecting the company's cybersecurity, for a number of Fortune 500 businesses, I have learned that the number one protection against cyber threats getting into your business or your personal life is to not let them in, in the first place.

Whether you visit a website, download an app, or receive a gift via email, somebody is getting something from you - it might be validation of your email address, pieces of your personal information, or access to your device - and it's really difficult to differentiate whether the purpose is noble or nefarious, or whether the activity is harmless or harmful.

It's patently clear that it's not good enough to just hear what the right thing to do is or what the wrong thing to avoid is, it must make sense and be real to each person.

In this book, and the successive books in this series, Sandra Estok uses her own unique brand of storytelling to make cybersecurity risks real and easy to understand for the reader. Her personal stories are filled with rich detail and life lessons that are relatable to anyone.

I met Sandra in 2012, and it was clear from the beginning she was a force on her own. As we interacted more over the years, I saw her grasp a fuller picture of cybersecurity and the overwhelming challenge of communicating concepts effectively and how readers can protect themselves and their families.

Eventually she came to work on my team and fully committed herself to the responsibility of helping others become aware of how to protect themselves from cybersecurity risks. As we delivered our cybersecurity messages on stages around the world, I watched her craft, deliver, and improve our message, and then repeat the cycle until the message was perfect.

Simply put, in two short years she developed the most effective and robust security awareness program I have ever seen. It was successful across languages and mediums, and influenced thousands to adopt safer cyber habits.

Today, Sandra is a compelling cybersecurity influencer and world class presenter, and I am excited to see her reach expand.

In *Happily Ever Cyber!* Sandra has utilized multiple teaching techniques to increase comprehension. You can engage the topics by searching your own life experience to identify relatable personal experiences to drive the learned point home, making the lesson last.

I appreciate that Sandra included a detailed glossary of key terms to ensure subjects are easy to understand, as well as a set of references for further learning that you can use to get more in-depth information on cybersecurity risks.

As the former President of ASIS International, the world's largest security management industry association, I have seen many people from around the world try and explain security in an accessible way, this book is a quick and easy read using unpretentious language for readers of any age and skill level.

As someone who worked with Sandra closely, her passion for the subject matter and for helping readers learn are clearly present in her development and writing of this book series.

Enjoy!

Dave Tyson, CPP, CISSP, MBA
Senior Vice President
Apollo Information Systems

Living Happily Ever Cyber!

A s the cyberworld expands, so does cybercrime. The possibility of our information being impacted by a hack or data breach is not a matter of "if" but "when."

Did you know that?

- there is an estimated 1 in 11.5 million chance of getting attacked by a shark
- there is an estimated 1 in 1 million chance of getting struck by lightning
- the odds of getting a hole in one in golf are 1 in 12,000 for an average golfer
- the odds of getting killed by a falling coconut are 1 in 50.7 million
- the odds of finding a pearl in an oyster are 1 in 12,000

Did you also know that? *(source details included in bibliography and references)*

- The odds for Americans to become a victim of cybercrime and identity theft are 1 in 4. (1)
- There are nearly four billion Internet users (nearly half of the world's population of 7.7 billion). (2)

- There is a cyber-attack every 39 seconds. (3)
- A ransomware attack occurs every 14 seconds. The prediction for ransomware impact cost is $20 billion worldwide.(3)
- 43% of data breaches occurred to small businesses, and within 6 months, 60% of them were out of business. (4)
- Every minute Cybercrime costs $2.9 million to the global economy (5)
- From 2020 to 2025 the expending on cybersecurity is estimated to exceed $1 trillion (2)
- 26+ billion is the number of IoT devices currently connected (things connected in the Internet) (5)
- The US is #8 among the top countries affected by Robocalls or Scam Calls with a total of 54 billion calls placed. Brazil is #1. (5)
- Nearly 1 in 5 people lost money due to Imposter Scams. The total fraud losses recorded by the FTC (Federal Trade Commission) were $1.48 billion in total. (5)
- The number of stolen records is 8,100 per minute. In 2019 at least 5.3 billion records have been exposed through data breaches. (5)
- 56% of the records stolen came from social media services. (5)
- Over 1 million children were a victim of identity theft or fraud, resulting in $2.6 billion in losses and costing families over $540 million in out-of-pocket expenses. (5)
- 65% of data breach incidents involved identity theft. (2)
- The top infected email theme and keyword is "Bill" and "Invoice" (6)
- There is a new victim of identity theft every two seconds! (6)

We may have heard of some of these statistics before in the news, on a website, or during a training class. All this information about cybersecurity gives us greater insight about cyber-attacks, identity theft, data breaches, privacy issues, scams and many other topics.

The reality is that our cyber world has dramatically changed. We rely on technology for everything we do, accessing information from anywhere and everywhere.

Children carry cell phones, and even use their sleeping parent's thumb (without their consent) to unlock their phone so the kids can get online or play games. People are trading in-person interactions for online ones, sharing a lot of information via social media platforms about themselves, their business, and families.

How dependent are you on the Internet today?

Are the topics of cybersecurity, cybercrime, and identity theft overwhelming to you?

Do you think about how easy it is for someone to get access to your information, your finances, or data, and steal it from you?

What do you do to keep yourself, your business, and your family safe from cyber threats?

Can you imagine being worry-free and feeling safe and happy as you interact with the cyberworld and live *Happily Ever Cyber*?

Using stories that relate and connect us at a personal level provides a more creative way to learn about cybersecurity, cybercrime, and identity theft. When you feel inspired and encouraged rather than intimidated by an overload of technical information, you will be empowered to take action.

Happily Ever Cyber! is the foundation of my cybersecurity book series and provides the basic answers to your questions about cybersecurity, cybercrime, and identity theft. It introduces and explains the dangers of the online world through personal stories.

This book series was written because the amount of information related to cybersecurity is overwhelming, full of technical terms, and not always clear regarding what actions to take. You will receive clear, simple, and direct answers to your questions about cybersecurity, cybercrime, and identity theft, and be inspired and encouraged to protect what matters most to you.

Congratulations on taking the first step. This book lays the foundation for what you will learn in this series and ensures success in your quest for greater cyber safety.

Many people want to run ahead and get to the action steps, "what to do and then move on." But that's not you. You understand that the *Why* is just as important as the *What* and the *How*. When you finish *Happily Ever Cyber!* you will be ready to dive deeper into the simple recommendations and practices in each book that follows in the series.

My goal with this book series is to change the way we perceive the cyberworld by making cybersecurity simple.

Although the seven stories I share are specific to my life, my adventures, how I grew up, and my choices, much later in life I discovered these stories are all connected to cybersecurity. With each story, my intention is to create a space for you to decide the What, Why and How to protect yourself against cyber threats.

I am also incorporating seven additional cyber stories, they are narrated and transcribed as it occurred to each of the amazing leaders I interviewed. Some of them are sharing their stories for the first time. The stories provide specific examples and different ways to illustrate how cybercrime and identity theft can happen. Each story follows with three recommendations and additional resources available for you.

My hope and dream are that these stories will inspire and encourage you to act and protect yourself against hackers, scammers and Cybermonsters.

Together, we embark on our journey to find your version of living *Happily Ever Cyber!*

When I was eleven years old, my family was evicted from the place we called "home" in Venezuela, my native country. The only house my family could afford to rent was a shack in the middle of the landlord's property. It was a rectangle box of concrete with a metal door, an uneven ceiling, and one small window in the front. There was no bathroom or water service inside, just a latrine in the middle of the yard. It was certainly different from the other nice family homes around us.

Every day, in front of the house, I watched kids playing volleyball. I never learned to play any sport. We always moved a lot and sports just couldn't be a priority in our family. Watching these kids made me dream of playing with them. However, they rejected me every time I asked. Then, one day, one of the kids yelled at me:

"Get out of here! You live in an ugly shack, loser. You are never going to make it. You will never be one of us."

As I was walking away, another kid said, "Hey, come back —of course you can play with us—a new game called "La Ollita."

In this game, the first person who dropped the ball would kneel in the center of the circle and everyone would hit that person with the ball.

Going home, my bruises hurt along with my broken pride. I wanted to cry, but instead, I remembered what my school teacher, Ms. Marleen said, "Happiness is a choice, because we are the architects of our own life."

That day, I promised myself that no matter the situation, I would always choose happiness and take action so my dreams could come true.

I declared, "I am going to learn to play volleyball!"

But first I needed to figure out how to make money to buy my own ball because playing "La Ollita" was not going to be the way to learn and join a volleyball team.

Based on that goal, I got my first job with a nearby family, helping their thirty-year-old daughter, Shelly, learn to read and write. Her mom promised to pay me based on results. Every day for the next four months, Shelly and I worked together.

Shelly wanted to read, write, and spell her name. We focused on achieving that by practicing the alphabet daily. I spent countless hours creating flash cards for Shelly so she could associate the letters with images. We repeatedly worked on writing and spelling her name.

Finally, the day came when Shelly could write and spell her name. We were both so excited! Though I was happy for her, I was also happy for myself. Finally, I would get paid and my dream of buying a ball and learning how to play volleyball would become reality.

Sitting at the elegant dining table, Shelly and I waited for her mom to arrive. I noticed the pretty chandelier hanging from the ceiling. Shelly's mom opened the embroidered wooden double door and entered the room.

Shelly started spelling her name and wrote it on a piece of paper. I was so proud. But her mom looked at me and said, "Is this all you have done for four months? What a waste! I am not paying you for this," and walked away. Shelly was devastated, and my dream of playing volleyball seemed to vanish.

I went home and cried for hours, but, remembering Ms. Marleen's quote and my promise to choose happiness, I decided to explore selling something.

"Mom, how do you make tamarind juice?"

There was a tamarind tree in our yard. I made the juice with the fruit and poured it into one side of a plastic bag, tied the corner, and froze it. Because of its shape, I made the sign, "Boobs for Sale."

A couple of weeks later, I had earned the equivalent of fifteen dollars and bought my first volleyball.

Every day after school, I practiced volleyball for hours against the front wall of our home. As I learned the basics, I joined a local team and got some coaching. Fast-forward five years: I was playing in many tournaments and our team even played in a national championship!

A month later, our landlord passed away, and his relatives came by our home and told us to "get out." We were being evicted again.

Our family packed up and went to live with my stepfather's family. At only sixteen years old, I had just graduated from high school. I enrolled in a government program to become a secretary to help my family while I considered pursuing further education.

I kept playing volleyball, and life started to get better when I got an internship at a prestigious global Fortune 500 company. One day, one of the executive's administrative assistants asked me, "Sandra, please go to this 'five-star' hotel and deliver this envelope."

The hotel's lobby was stunning and luxurious. The floor was tiled with polished marble. There was a gorgeous chandelier in the center of the high ceiling, and a sophisticated flower arrangement adorned the side. I had no idea that places like this one existed, except in movies. The concierge walked me over to the restaurant area. As I handed the envelope to the man who was waiting, he said, "Sandra, have a seat. Order breakfast and charge it to my room," and walked away.

For a moment, I stood there speechless, but finally decided to sit and eat. There was so much food!

As I was enjoying the feast, people started showing up for breakfast; some in business attire and carrying briefcases. At one of the tables, I saw a woman using a small computer. This world was very different from mine.

As I continued to observe everyone, my mind started to visualize myself wearing a suit, carrying a briefcase with a small computer, traveling, and making an impact in the world. From this point on, a new life of possibilities opened up in front of me. I thought of my mom and my little brother at home and how they were counting on me. Then I declared, "I am going to become a businesswoman. I just need to figure out how to pay for my night school college degree."

During the next seven years, I was fully dedicated to completing my English, Information Technology, and System Engineering degrees all while working and rotating through better positions in several multinational companies.

I started my career as an intern secretary, just months after I finished high school. Then I continued to advance until the last global organization I worked for transferred me and my family to the United States. We moved to the Midwest and started our new life of possibilities.

Over the course of my career, I have worked for public and private multinational companies. I have had the privilege of managing and leading the implementation of several programs, building teams, and delivering key business initiatives in the Information Technology (IT) area for Latin America, the United States, and Europe. I switched my career from IT and started in the cybersecurity industry and, much later, in the Data Privacy sector.

I have achieved almost every one of my dreams, and sometimes, even more than I dreamed of! by always remembering Ms. Marleen's words that "happiness is a choice" and by taking action with the belief that we are the architects of our own lives.

There is an immense sense of gratitude for all the blessings I have received. My life is full of realities that "once upon a time" were only in my mind because I never believed others could limit how far I could go.

One of my favorite quotes is from the movie Rocky VI, when Rocky talks to his son about life. He says, "It ain't about how hard you hit, it's about how hard you can get hit and keep moving forward; how much you can take and keep moving forward. That's how winning is done."

Throughout my journey, there was always someone—a kid, familiar or unknown person, a boss, co-worker, or even an employee — pushing me around or bullying me. As a result of those moments, I grew the most in every aspect of my life, including my confidence, by confronting my fears in my most vulnerable and darkest times.

"Well, there's one thing: they can't order me to stop dreaming."

— Charles Perrault - Cinderella

Today, choosing happiness continues to be the focus of my life, my family, my health, my relationships, and my business. Founding my own company, Way2Protect, becoming a speaker, and writing the *Happily Ever Cyber!* book series allows me to fulfill my promise and act on my dream to change the way cybersecurity and our cyberworld is perceived.

I trust that you will enjoy this journey together as we embark on our quest to live *Happily Ever Cyber!*

Sandra

The Deep Blue Ocean

When we receive an email from our friends with a cool link to click on, most of the time cyber-attacks, data breaches, and identity theft are not in the forefront of our minds.

The reality is, sometimes the person who sent the information may not really be our friend. Our computer may get infected, we start seeing weird pop-up messages, the computer is opening random pages or responding very slow. Once our computer is fixed, if the impact was minor, we may forget until the next time we get another "cool" link to click on.

We also ignore cybersecurity issues when being immersed in social media. We start posting, liking, or simply browsing and clicking on ads. We might not see the consequences right away, but our information may have just gotten into the wrong hands and we do not even realize it yet.

We might not think about cybersecurity when we are in a public place and we cannot wait to use the free Wi-Fi or download something free. Our information, data, or identity could be stolen. Unfortunately, we are clueless until it is too late, and we have to start the painful recovery process.

We may not think about cybersecurity, identity theft or cyber-crime because in our minds it cannot happen to us, or it seems too hard or too technical. We decide it is better not to do anything.

Sometimes, when our information has been compromised in a recent hack or data breach we have seen on the news, we may not even know that we should take action and change our password, cancel our credit card, or review our credit report to check if everything is in order with our information. And if it has been compromised, we may not know how to take the necessary actions to minimize the damage.

Even if we have been a victim of a personal cyber incident in the past and if it was painful recovering the information or fixing the situation, it is still not enough for us to change our habits and how we perceive cybersecurity to protect what matters most to us. Have you ever wondered why?

According to Cybersecurity Ventures, (2) "Cybercriminal activity is one of the biggest challenges that humanity will face in the next two decades. Cyber-attacks are the fastest growing crime globally and they are increasing in size, sophistication, and cost."

What is Cybercrime?

Cybercrime is a criminal activity involving your computer, phone, or any other electronic or network device as well as your email, and social media accounts. These crimes could be in the form of fraud, sale of illicit drugs, pornography, or weapons. Cybercrime may also be malicious software to hack or harm other people, money laundering, or extortion. Or in the form of identity theft using your personal information without your permission or impersonating you to conduct criminal acts on your behalf, and so much more.

All the facts and statistics we previously covered are alarming, and yes, very scary. But there are many things that we all can do to reduce the chance of becoming a victim of cybercrime and identity theft. They are not all about bits and bytes. In some cases, they are habits that could simplify and protect your cyber world and with practice they can become second nature to you, this is part of our journey together to live *Happily Ever Cyber!*

Do you look both ways before you cross a street?

Do you stick your fingers or metal objects into an electricity outlet?

As kids we learned the basics of crossing a street or handling an electrical outlet and now, they are second nature to our safety. Similarly, there are actions we can take to protect our daily lives when we travel, use our phone, email, or social media channels, and other cyber activities.

There are other actions that might require more guidance, tools, and details for you to apply, but again, we are not only talking about technical changes you need to implement. This foundational book covers What we can do and Why. The rest of the books in the *Happily Ever Cyber!* series focus on How. However, we included a checklist chapter in this book, for those of you who want to start taking action right away to protect your cyber world.

My commitment to you is to continue speaking and writing engaging content to simplify cybersecurity and guide you in how to protect what matters most to you against hackers, scammers and Cybermonsters.

This book contains seven chapters, as follows:

Chapter 1 covers who are Cybermonsters, what do they want to steal from us and why they are motivated to hack. This chapter explains why cybercrime or identity theft can happen to me, you, or all of us.

Chapter 2 explains what the top areas of concern are with our passwords, what password managers are, and what to consider when selecting one.

Chapter 3 covers what are the top areas of concern for our online information connecting physical security and cybersecurity and why be cautious with "Free" offers.

Chapter 4 describes why it is important to get guidance from someone with the skills and expertise we need. Why it is important to do a self-assessment to figure out where our skills are and what we have to do to get better and achieve what we want. And why it is important to have a plan or recommendation to follow in our practice, so the learning, skills, and new habits become second nature to us.

Chapter 5 provides a high-level view of the *Happily Ever Cyber!* book series. For example, there will be a specific book about what to do if you become a victim of identity theft and the resources you need to recover from it. These books are all about how you can protect yourself, your business, and your family, and reduce the chances of becoming a victim of cybercrime or identity theft. In this chapter, you will have the opportunity to do your own personal cyber self-assessment.

Chapter 6 includes a cyber checklist you can use as a guide to start your journey to protect your information from hackers, scammers, and Cybermonsters.

Chapter 7 provides you a set of cyber stories from victims of identity theft or cybercrime. This is an opportunity for you to learn from their experiences, whether you have been a victim or not of identity theft or cybercrime. If these stories relate to you or someone you know it is also an opportunity to reflect upon because we are the only ones who can take control of our cyber world so we can live *Happily Ever Cyber!*

At the end of this first book, there is a glossary of common terms in the cyberworld and an additional list of online resources with tips you can use to protect your personal information, your family, finances, business, or anything that matters most to you and my long term vision for the *Happily Ever Cyber!* foundation.

Are you ready to continue with our journey?
What is your biggest fear?
How would your life be different without this fear?
Are you ready to face your cybersecurity fears?

"If you are ever near the water, you are going to die," my mom repeated this phrase over and over to me during most of my life, and I never learned how to swim. How could I even try? I thought I would die.

When my mom was in high school, one of her friends was drowning in a swimming pool. My mom froze and was unable to do anything to help her friend. Her friend died.

I never learned how to swim because I didn't have access to a pool or swimming lessons and because my mom wanted to shield me from drowning.

When I was 21 years old, I was working at another Fortune 500 multinational company and my friends from the office planned a weekend getaway. I wanted to go. The only problem was we had to ride in a motorboat to get to the destination. Because I wanted to fit in so badly, I accepted the invitation. It turned out to be one of the worst moments of fear in my life.

I returned determined that one day I would conquer this fear. It just wouldn't be that day. Not being ready to confront the situation and busy with working and going to school at night, I recited all the reasons why it was not the right moment to conquer this fear.

Six years later, I was working at another global consumer packaged goods (CPG) company in Information Technology, responsible for the Andean Countries which included Venezuela, Colombia, Ecuador, and Peru. One day, I was invited to join a group in the office to get certified in scuba diving.

I thought, "What a great opportunity to conquer my fear of the water, to explore the ocean, and to be part of the cool group at my new job. Yes, I can do it."

I asked the scuba diving instructor, Jorge, if I needed to know how to swim to take the PADI Open Water Diver certification.

He said, "No worries, Sandra, you are not going to do any swimming strokes down there. Scuba diving is very relaxing. It will be the most beautiful thing you will ever see in your life."

"Well, if that is the case," I said, "sign me up!"

Among the twelve co-workers who joined the adventure, there were eight beginners and four seasoned and certified divers.

During the next two weeks, we completed the theory classes required for the certification that consisted of learning the basic principles of scuba diving, the physics, physiology, diving equipment, dive planner, environment, and the diving skills needed.

The next step in the certification process was to develop and practice the basic scuba diving skills in a pool. The final test consisted of four immersion dives over two days in the open water of the ocean.

I learned about the risks of practicing scuba diving, including decompression sickness, also known as DCS, arterial air embolism, drowning, and nitrogen narcosis. I couldn't stop thinking and asking Jorge about the sharks. I was very worried about a shark eating me.

We all went to the local gym where an indoor swimming pool was available. I put on my rental equipment and went to the pool.

During the first exercise, Jorge explained, "You need to float for two minutes in the pool."

As I took my first step on the stairs to go into the pool, my heart started racing. It felt like my heartbeat was almost pushing my heart out of my chest. My stomach was cramping, and I had a weird sweating sensation. Soaking wet, I was not even in the water yet.

I felt like I was going to faint. But then I remembered how much I wanted to fit into this group, and I kept going.

We were in the deepest end of the pool with everyone floating in the middle of the pool. They were all very relaxed except for me.

I couldn't stop holding onto the safety ledge of the pool. There was no way I was going to let go. My feet could not touch the bottom of the pool.

The two minutes were up, and the nightmare was finally over.

"Wait a minute, now we have to do a bunch of exercises under the water... What have I done?"

The mandatory exercises and practices in the pool consisted of how to learn the basics of scuba diving and how to best react in stressful situations. Some of the exercises required taking off your mask, taking the water out of it, or taking the air regulator off your mouth and purging it. Also, we needed to learn how to share a single air regulator and alternate with a partner in case of an emergency, among many other exercises.

I did my best under the circumstances trying to forget my mom's words, "If you are in the water, you are going to die." I failed most of the time.

As I was sitting on the bottom of the pool and looking up at the water over me, I was unable to take my mask off. I could not take the regulator air from my mouth and alternate it with a partner as part of the practice exercises everyone else was doing. Totally overwhelmed and freaked out, I had to constantly go up to the surface.

At the end of the session, Jorge pulled me aside and said, "Sandra, no worries. Most people are very stressed out while practicing in the swimming pool. Once you get in the ocean and you see the most beautiful thing in the world, you won't be so scared anymore. Besides, your partner is going to be Al. He is a Master Scuba Diver and the most experienced member of our group."

Al was also the head of our Human Resources department. As I was relatively new to the organization, having Al as my partner was not working to calm my nerves.

With Jorge's promise that I would see the most beautiful thing in the world, I was excited for our upcoming open water test.

That day arrived and we were at the ocean. For the next two days, we were going to test to earn our scuba diving PADI certification. I put the suit on, and stood on the shore looking at the waves. It was so beautiful: the blue ocean, the sun shining, the breeze touching my face. It was warm but very pleasant. However, my heart knew what was about to come, and the beating fest started all over again.

Jorge explained, "Our first dive won't require you to do any exercises. It is just our first immersion to fall in love with scuba diving. You are going to see something magnificent, the most beautiful thing in the world. Now you just need to swim 65 feet to our immersion point, where you see that rock, it is called 'La Piedra de la Lavandera' (The Washer Stone). Our adventure will start there."

"We'll be swimming WHAT?"

The BC/BCD, Buoyancy Compensator or Buoyancy Control Device, also known as the stabilizer, stab jacket, or wing is an essential part of the scuba diving gear and it is part of the diver's life support equipment. The primary function is to control buoyancy and hold the tank during the diving. They are designed with an inflatable bladder. You control the volume of air and this allows you to stay above the water. Since I did not have to worry about my head being above the water, I just needed to figure out how to move my body to get to the point of immersion. "How hard could it be?"

While trying to get there, the water was in my eyes and my mouth. The waves were creating so much resistance. And worse than that, I knew I could not touch the floor anymore. "Oh no!" Everyone else was already at the immersion point and I had only advanced about three feet.

Al came over and held my hand and started pulling me until we reached the immersion point. "Don't worry, I've got you," he said. "I will hold your hand the whole time. Eileen is also coming with us. The three of us will have a blast."

Eileen was an intern in the Human Resources department who had also joined the organization recently like me. I barely heard what Al said, as my chest was beating fast and I was sweating, thinking, "Come on, how could anyone be sweating this much in the water?"

Time to go down! Al started to deflate his BCR. I did exactly what he was doing. I grabbed his hand with no intention of letting go.

We were about 15-20 ft. under the water. Everyone was moving their fins so much that the only thing I could see was blurred water and sand.

Al grabbed Eileen's hand and now the three of us started our immersion to fall in love with diving.

My mask was getting water inside and my vision was blurry.

"I must focus. I am not going to die."

Only a few minutes had passed. I was holding Al's hand tightly. I was on his right side while Eileen was holding his other hand. I am not sure how, but Al's diving regulator, the thing that pushes the flowing-air so he could breathe, came off his mouth.

Al was very calm. He let Eileen's hand go and then he tried to let go of my hand, too. But I couldn't let him go. I thought that if I did that I would die.

Al was pointing with his left index finger at his mouth and I shook my head, "No, no…"

I'm thinking, "What the heck! Why does he want me to take the regulator off my mouth?! I don't want to practice now."

He kept pointing and trying to release my hand, but I tightened my grip and kept shaking my head, "NO."

Al used his left hand and with his leg kicked the hose on his right side and grabbed the spare regulator, also called the "octopus", and put the air back in his mouth. And we went up. Al was very angry. "Uh oh"… Al yelled at me because he was out of air and could have died!

"How could you do this? Didn't you see that I needed my right hand to put the air back in my mouth?"

After we got back from the first immersion, I started throwing up for a long time. I blamed it on breakfast but deep down I knew what was going on.

I wanted to quit. The thought of going back in the water four more times to do all the required exercises to be certified was tormenting me. "I cannot do this."

Then I commented, "I don't feel well. I am going to skip the rest of the activities and wait for all of you at the hotel."

Al made eye contact with me and shouted, "Get your rear end back to the water. You are not a quitter. You are going to do each of the exercises and get that certification, are we clear?"

"Yes, sir," is all I could say.

I completed each of the mandatory exercises and did the four required immersions, throwing up each time in between.

We finally did it. I was a certified scuba diver.

In the car while driving back, we were all talking about the amazing weekend and everyone was smiling and chatting. Al suddenly pointed out how sore his right arm was. In fact, he said, "I am not able to move my arm at all."

And it hit him right there, he looked at me, "Sandra, I was pulling you all over the whole time. Why didn't you move your legs?"

And I responded, "Oh, Al, I don't know how to swim."

Far out in the ocean, where the water is as blue as the prettiest cornflower, and as clear as crystal, it is very, very deep; so deep, indeed."
*   - Hans Christian Andersen - The Little Mermaid*

The ocean is vast and full of beautiful things to enjoy. We can sail, navigate, swim, and see its amazing sea life, and so much more. We can also encounter dangerous things that are either internal and/or external elements of the ocean that could endanger our lives and the lives of others.

Oceanographers, scientists who study the ocean, divide it into layers taking into consideration the physical characteristics of the water like the density, temperature, and amount of light within each layer. Research (7) shows the ocean is categorized into three layers:

-   The surface ocean or epipelagic zone: This layer is warmer and refers to the top 660 feet of the ocean where light penetrates. The transition into the deep ocean happens when the water temperature drops and the density increases. This is called thermocline.

- The deep ocean or mesopelagic and bathypelagic zone: This layer is colder and denser than the surface, the distance extends up to 13,000 feet. The temperature is generally between 32-37.4 F°.
- The very deep or abyssopelagic and hadalpelagic zone: This layer extends from 13,000 feet below the surface to the sea floor.

Can you imagine what could have happened if Al was not a Master Scuba Diver who managed to control the situation? Clearly, I didn't have the skills, nor did I know the fundamentals required to be a scuba diver.

I risked a person's life because I underestimated the dangers of the ocean and scuba diving. I did not recognize how important it was to get to know the basics, understand Why, What, and How things happen, so I could have made the right decisions and choices to protect myself and those around me.

The depth of the ocean with all of its nuances compares to the Internet today. We can find amazing things online that make our lives so much easier. We communicate with each other. We navigate, conduct business, and pursue our education. We can find and resolve health matters, explore infinite adventures and possibilities, and so much more.

Just because we know how to use social media, use our phone, click on links, manage our email, and browse online, it doesn't mean that we know everything to safely navigate the Internet ocean. There are many dangers that we need to be aware of, for example, what and when not to click, and what to do if one of our clicks triggers an imminent potential risk to be a victim of identity theft or cybercrime. We need to know how to minimize the damage if we fall into a trap and our cyber world is compromised.

With scuba diving, one thing is to know the basics and fundamentals, but also to know what and how to protect ourselves, our businesses, and our families to keep them from drowning in the Cyber ocean.

The Internet ocean is deep - we can't get there just by swimming or taking a speedboat. Once you're there, you'll realize that, like the ocean, the Internet is also divided into three layers:

- The surface web: Refers to the Internet we all know and navigate to connect with family, friends, and businesses, where people read information in websites, watch videos, do their banking, use social media, play games, do shopping, and may pursue many more online interests. It is estimated that the indexed web contains at least 5.62 billion pages (8). Indexing refers to the various processes of adding web page content into a search engine such as Google, Yahoo, or Bing to find the information we are looking for on the Internet. For example, "where to buy a volleyball" or "the best scuba diving destinations."

- The deep web: Refers to the Internet that is not indexed. In order to access these pages, you need to know the exact link or details to get to the website. To use the deep web, you need a special browser, such as TOR (The Onion Router) which is the most popular portal. Using the TOR browser could raise suspicion as your Internet provider can't see what you are doing, and is not a browser for regular Internet use, consider this for informational purposes only. TOR was developed in the mid-1990s by the United States Navy. The deep web includes legitimate content that is hidden from search engines because the information is not intended for public consumption and you can access this content using a specific username and password.

  For example, law enforcement communications, academic information, banking portals, scientific reports and Internet sites or databases of major companies. The deep web can be used as a communication resource and sharing of information for good or bad intentions. Because of its anonymity factor, communications to avoid surveillance or the tracking of Internet habits and whistleblowing situations are also common.

The deep web may be 500 times larger than the surface web, according to estimates in the cybersecurity industry. The depth of the deep web is more than we can ever imagine, and it gets more dangerous the deeper you get.

- The dark web: Technically, the dark web is also part of the deep web, but much deeper, and unless you know exactly where to go you can't get there. There may still be legitimate content that occurs in the dark web to circumvent surveillance measures. Cybercrime and many illicit activities also happen in this layer of the Internet ocean.

When you hear about the latest data breach with millions of records stolen, do you know what it means?

In the dark web, there is a market, an entire e-commerce system developed to sell drugs, guns, counterfeit money, and documents. Other practices include, human trafficking, fake college degrees, fake coupons, child abuse, hacking forums, and most of the stolen records in data breaches.

There is a price tag for your credit and debit card numbers, for your social security number, your social media user and password accounts, your subscription services credentials for example in Spotify, Hulu, Netflix, and many other, to your reward programs for airlines and hotels, to your email address and password, your banking account data, your healthcare information including your medical records and insurance information, and other sensitive information that has value when someone tries to impersonate you with the purpose to steal your money.

The more personal information stolen about you, the higher the price tag to resell in the dark web. For example, your stolen credit card or financial account information packaged with your name, your address, answer to your security questions, your social security number and any additional sensitive information would cost more than just selling your credit card number because the more information available about you, the easier it is to steal your identity and impersonate you to pursue illicit activities or have access to everything you own.

The dark web is estimated to be a tiny fraction of the deep web. It is also unreliable and plagued with fake domains. Many scams occur there as curious people try to venture there and navigate these dangerous waters.

Similar to the ocean layers, there are not marked lines to each of these web layers.

The next chapter begins exploring who uses the dark web, what are the techniques used for cybercrime and identity theft, and why they could happen to me, happen to you - happen to all of us.

As the dive into the Internet ocean continues, there's no need to worry. I've got your hand. We are on this journey together.

Chapter 1

Are There Really Monsters Under Your Bed?

Were you ever afraid of the dark? Did you believe the "bogey-man" or "el coco" existed and it was coming for you?

When I was a kid, I developed a technique to keep the monsters or "el coco" away and unable to get to me. I would sneak into my mom's bed in the middle of the night. As long as I touched my mom with my two hands and my left foot, I believed I was protected. Nobody could take me away and the monsters could not scare me anymore.

What was your technique to keep the monsters away?
How big were your monsters?
Did they have teeth?
Were they loud or did they whisper to you?

We have grown up and the monsters under the bed don't scare us anymore, they aren't real. Well, for most of us... I confess I still put my hands and left foot on my husband's body, just in case.

"The world seems full of good men, even if there are monsters in it."

– Bram Stoker, Dracula.

Nowadays, there are other types of monsters that hide behind a keyboard, I call them Cybermonsters and they are real! Some of them are big, they can be anywhere and could be very dangerous. Others pretend to be "our grandma", when in reality, they are the wolf that wants to eat us.

Who are the Cybermonsters?

Let's look at who are the Cybermonsters that exist in the cyber-world and what is their intent.

"CyCri-M0" - The Cyber Criminal Monsters – They have over-taken the drug trade and they are the most profitable illegal industry at this time; they go after one thing: our money.

For CyCri-M0, it is all about profits. They are well organized like a business. They may even have Monday meetings to discuss the objectives of the week and how much information they need to steal to meet their quota. These Cybermonsters are big. They can be very powerful and like any business, they have different ways to source and obtain their product: YOU!

They also employ different resources (hackers) with technical capabilities to conduct their business or they might purchase the information once somebody else has stolen it.

"HaKi-M0" - The Hacktivist Monster – This could be an individual or a group that has some sort of social or political mission.

The word "hacktivist" is the combination of "activists" who are individuals that promote, impede, direct, or intervene in social, political, economic, or environmental causes with the desire to make changes in society; combined with the word "hacking" which means gaining unauthorized access to data and systems.

Some examples include believing in the freedom of information, human rights, or expressing their opposition to something they believe is wrong.

HaKi-M0 is equipped with the same tools and techniques as CyCri-M0 Monsters but because their goal is to disrupt or bring attention to a specific cause, there is no financial gain. They have a desire to humiliate and embarrass their victims.

"InSi-M0" - The Insider Monster – These are individuals with legitimate access to your personal information or your business' data they could be employees, former employees, contractors, vendors or business partners, vengeful spouses, or anyone else - whether by accident, because of ignorance or negligence, or even for a specific financial or malicious intent, could misuse the access and negatively affect you, your organization or business operation.

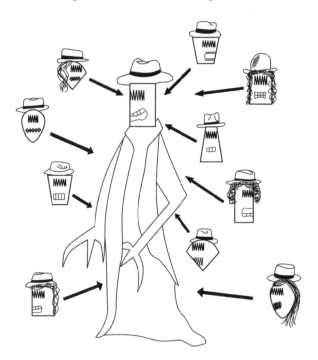

The InSi-M0 knows your business, your data, and in some cases, they know the methods you use to protect your information.

The InSi-M0 may be involved with espionage, fraud, theft, or the disclosure of unauthorized information, sabotage of your systems or operations, etc.

"NaSu-M0" - The Nation State Cybermonsters – They are motivated by political, economic, technical, or military agendas. They work to disrupt a specific target, either a country or government, organizations, or individuals to gain access to valuable information. As they work to build up their own economics or businesses, or they may use stolen intellectual property or valuable information hacked from companies and governments.

The NaSu-M0's target has shifted in the last few years toward individual consumers and small businesses because just like other Cybermonsters, they look for vulnerable and easy entry points to steal critical data.

Because NaSu-M0s are supported by their states, they have no fear of legal retribution. They are huge Cybermonsters sometimes with unlimited resources at their disposal.

What do Cybermonsters want from us?

As we described the type of Cybermonsters and what motivates them, we are going to explore further what they really want from us and what techniques they could use to get it.

Personal Information from You or your Clients/Customers

Your personal information or what you store for your customers is commonly categorized as your account and password, social security or your ID information, name, address, and other identifiable information. However, there is less common information, such as your favorite sport, your parents' names, school or pet information, your location of birth, etc. that can be used to gain access to your accounts and impersonate you easily.

Financial Information

This type of information refers to your credit card numbers, your bank account information, your retirement plans or 401K, taxes, and returns. It could also be your electronic funds transfer account or other similar accounts that are targeted for the sole purpose of stealing your money.

Health Information

This information is commonly used in identity theft and insurance fraud to make fake claims. Health records are very valuable to Cybermonsters because it is one more piece of data, they can use to impersonate you. Medical history records may be used to blackmail or publicly humiliate victims.

Your Business's Intellectual Property or Trade Secrets

What would be the consequences to your business if Cybermonsters were to steal your business methods, strategies, intellectual property, plans, forecasts, market analysis, and other details used to operate your business?

This information could be sold to your competition or they could duplicate your business model. The Cybermonsters could be working for your organization as employees, contractors, or vendors.

What are the techniques Cybermonsters use for cybercrime?

Let's explore what the different types of cybercrime techniques are that Cybermonsters use:

Malware

Cybermonsters use malicious software, programs, or files known as "malware" with the intention of harming your computer or devices. There are many types of malware including viruses, worms, trojan horses, keyloggers, and spyware. The AV-TEST institute.org registers 350,000 malware creations every day.

One business model Cybermonsters use when they create malware is to sell it to the highest bidder on the dark web.

There is a booming black-market criminal service called Malware-as-a-Service (MaaS). It is an entire ecosystem to let the buyer acquire, implement, and profit from the malware. This is an imitation of Cloud services models known as Software-as-a-Service (SaaS) or Platform-as-a-Service (PaaS), etc.

Just like you do not produce the electricity in your house or own the equipment that generates it, and you pay the power company what you consume every month, cloud services deliver on-demand computer services either applications, computer resources or storage/backup services where you can have all your data or process transactions and you pay as you use these services.

Social Engineering

Cybermonsters use techniques to trick, manipulate, influence, convince, or deceive someone into divulging information or giving them control over a computer or devices in order to carry out their malicious intentions. Cybermonsters impersonate someone else. They may promise something of value or to help you, or they could threaten you so you give in to revealing your secret information.

Have you ever received a phone call from technical support claiming your computer was infected and that you needed to give them your user-name and password for them to help you?

Have you ever received a phone call that you needed to immediately contact a phone number because your Social Security or your IRS taxes were in jeopardy?

Have you ever received an email from a prince asking you to help with his inheritance and he would share the money with you in exchange for you providing your bank information?

If you answered "yes" to any of the questions above, someone has tried to take advantage of your human nature.

Let's explore the two common social engineering techniques: Phishing and Ransomware.

Phishing

While fishing is the activity of trying to catch fish, some of the techniques used include hooking and trapping. Also using bait to lure animals to catch or trap them. Phishing is the activity of trying to catch "you." Similar to fishing, the techniques include bait to lure you and catch or trap you.

Most phishing bait lives in your inbox when you get an email from your bank, credit card company, official agencies, or other institutions asking you to verify your identity or provide your credentials by clicking on a malicious link or an infected attachment.

Cybermonsters could also try to phish you through voice calls, texts, and social media.

There are many different types of phishing. We will cover the two major methods below:

Deceptive Phishing

This is the most common type of phishing. Cybermonsters gain access to email lists and send large amounts of phony emails attempting to obtain confidential information from anyone who falls for it, by clicking or opening the infected links or attachments. The intention is to steal money from you or launch other cyber-attacks.

Spear Phishing

It targets specific individuals rather than a wide group of random people. Cybermonsters often research social media channels or other sites where you include personal information. The intention is to customize the communication to appear authentic and get you to click.

For a business, phishing is usually the first step Cybermonsters use to carry out a targeted cyber-attack. When they trick your employees to click or open a malicious link or infected file, giving Cybermonsters access to your network.

Ransomware

We all hope to never see a pop-up window on our computer screens with the message: "All your files are encrypted. To get the key to decrypt your files you have to pay $$$$$. You have 48 hours to do it. If you don't pay, all your files will be destroyed."

Ransomware is used as a form of extortion. Today it is one of the greatest dangers of the cyberworld since many of us keep our sensitive data on our computers or devices. It features a malware, or a computer program designed to lock/encrypt and deny access to your information. This encryption is unbreakable, meaning we are unable to get our files back on our own.

Ransomware mostly occurs via email, but it could also happen through compromised or insecure websites. It can lock or encrypt all kinds of files you have on your computer which means that pictures, videos, and other files may be impacted.

There are two types of ransomware:

Screen Lock-Ransomware

Your computer or device becomes a hostage. The screen gets locked and you can't access or manipulate your computer. The ransom message requests a fee to be paid for your computer to be freed up.

As the objective is to prevent you from accessing your computer, most of the time your files and system remain untouched. This type of ransomware uses techniques to pressure you into paying because it masquerades as law enforcement authorities and claims to issue fines if you don't do so.

Crypto-Ransomware

This form of ransomware is very harmful because it encrypts all the files or data on your computer, phone, or device and then it mixes up the name of your files and adds different extensions. It is hard to know what data has been impacted. This type of ransomware makes sure that you are unable to restore the files from your backup by deleting them.

In both types of ransomware, the request payment is made in bitcoins or other crypto currencies. Electronic cash is fast, reliable, and makes the tracing of illicit activities more difficult. Cybermonsters could use "mixing coin services" that pose as intermediaries to break the link between the sender and receiver. Cybermonsters hold the decryption key until the ransom is paid, that is if the key exists at all. And even if you pay, there is no guarantee your data will be restored, or later you might be asked for more money.

For businesses, a big concern of ransomware is that it could spread to all the other computers connected on your network. This would increase the damage to your operation or even disrupt your entire company. In some cases, Cybermonsters can exfiltrate your data including usernames, passwords, email addresses, personal information, and any other sensitive data. Encrypting your files for money might not be the only thing Cybermonsters are after.

Botnet Attacks

An Internet bot is created to perform simple and repetitive tasks faster than humans. For example, a bot allows Internet search engine companies to analyze millions of websites' data and files globally, and give us instant results every time we search for something on the Internet such as choosing a restaurant or selecting the best scuba diving gear!

The word Botnet is a blend of the words Robot and Network. They are a group or string of connected computers coordinated to perform repetitive tasks. However, Monsters use botnets with bad intentions by infecting a group of computers and controlling them remotely. Like a swarm of robots, they perform unison tasks like stealing information, sending spam, ad fraud, mining crypto currencies, targeting payment point of sale systems, or launching cyber-attacks on other computers. Cybermonsters do not steal your information, they steal your computer or devices' technical resources or power. The more devices that are compromised, the more power Cybermonsters have under their control.

Your servers, computers, mobile devices, or Internet-connected devices known as the Internet-of-Things (IoT) could be infected and be part of a botnet without your knowledge, as the installation would remain dormant until it is called upon to perform the intended action.

Browser Hijacking

This refers to when unwanted or unauthorized software is installed and alters your Internet browser used to navigate online.

Browser hijacking is typically used for advertising fraud but it could also be used to steal your information by taking you into websites to enter your personal information including your user ID, password, full name, address, social security number, financial information, and even the answers to your security questions. The purpose of browser hijacking could also be to spy on your browser search or display persistent ads for you to buy something.

Identity theft

Identity theft can happen to anyone, regardless of who you are, where you are from, or what you do for a living. It occurs when Cybermonsters use your personal information like your name, ID, or credit card number without your permission to commit fraud and other crimes. It could also happen through your social media accounts, your email, or mobile phone.

Identity theft is not just about your name. When someone impersonates you, they could have access to everything you own, your business, your personal finances, and your family.

Can it happen to me, to you, to us?

Have you ever lost something valuable or precious to you?

What were the consequences of your loss?

How did you feel?

I was returning from visiting my mom in Colombia, when the pilot said, "Folks, welcome to Miami. We have Homeland Security agents boarding. Please take out your passports."

As I handed my passport with my work visa to the agent, he said, "You are coming with us" … And they walked me, just me, off the plane and threw me into a room…yes, "that room."

I missed my connecting flight. My husband was waiting for me in Chicago and he didn't know where I was. Ten hours later, I was allowed to call him:

"Honey…"

Finally, they handed my passport to me with a big red stamp; "Revoked."

A few weeks later, I was back in Venezuela, my home country, and supported by my former employer's attorneys, I was processing a new visa. During the interview, they keep asking me questions about China; "Why were you in China? Who do you know in China? Who is your contact?"

"I don't know why you are asking me about China. I have never been there or anywhere in Asia."

"Well, somehow a smuggler in China got a hold of your information and has been smuggling women into the United States using your identity."

They hand me my new visa. I got a new passport, and everything is okay now.

Two weeks later, I am returning from Europe. We land and I get off the plane. At passport control, I hand my passport to the agent.

And he marched me right back into "that room", because I had to prove I was the "real" me. For six years this happened to me, every time I traveled.

When I "googled" my name, everything was in Chinese characters. There were several import and export companies, between Asia and Latin America that were using my name as their business name with the LTD at the end.

Can you believe that nobody wanted to travel with me? Not even my own husband!

Finally, I got my United States citizenship and passport. I changed my name, and everything is *really* okay now.

"I can't go back to yesterday because I was a different person then."

– Lewis Carroll, Alice in Wonderland

Identity theft and cybercrime can happen to anyone, regardless of who you are, where you are from, and what you do for a living. If you think that it won't happen to you because your company is too small, or you are not a famous person or because you do not go online or have a social media account, think again. Even without an active online life, you could be impersonated and/or your information can be stolen.

As we will explore in the next chapters, identity theft or cybercrime can happen through your social media accounts, your email, phone, when you write your personal sensitive information on a paper form or when you hand your credit card to someone. And as you already know from the statistics, there is a new victim of identity theft every two seconds.

Cybermonsters can steal more than just your identity. They could impersonate you and have access to everything you own. However, there are many steps that you and I can do together to reduce the chances of you becoming a victim of cybercrime and to protect what matters most to you.

Just keep reading!

Summary

We have explored the facts and statistics of cybercrime and that the odds in America of becoming a victim are 1 in 4 people.

We briefly navigated the Internet layers. We learned about the surface web, the deep, and the dark web. We discussed that the Internet we know may be 500 times smaller than the Internet that exists, and that the deep and dark web can be used for good or bad intentions.

As we complete this chapter, we know who the Cybermonsters are: "CyCri-M0" is motivated by financial gain; "HaKi-M0" follows a particular cause; "InSi-M0" lives inside our business, and "Na-Su-M0" are huge Cybermonsters with unlimited resources.

We also know what they want from us.

We have also learned the techniques they use to steal our information and that cybercrime or identity theft can happen to anyone- it happened to me -and could also happen to you.

Now it is your turn!

What Cybermonsters are you familiar with? Describe one situation that you or someone that you know has ever had with a Cybermonster. If this has never happened to you, think about a movie, TV program or news related to cyber criminals and describe the characteristics of the Cybermonster.

Is there anything related to cybercrime or identity theft that has happened to you or anyone you know? What did you do? If your answer is "No," check the news for the latest hack and imagine your information has been compromised. What would you do?

List five things that you care the most about, that you would do anything to protect:

1.	
2.	
3.	
4.	
5.	

Notes

What are the big takeaways for you in this chapter?

Chapter 2

———— ✑ ————

The D@msel 1n D T0wer

Do you remember your first kiss? Who was the person? Where were you? And how do you feel remembering that moment?

My mom was a tough cookie. She got pregnant as a teenager and my mom didn't want the same thing happening to me. Mom was very protective and guarded me like a hawk, she used to say: "cuidadito, mucho cuidadito con los varones" ("careful, very careful with the boys"). I was not allowed to have a boyfriend or hang out with boys. My mom always promised she would hunt me down if she knew a boy was near me.

Julius was a cute boy, with a muscular body, the most perfect hair, mesmerizing eyes, and his voice could make me melt by just saying "hi." We were both 14 years old and I had a crush on Julius. One day he kissed me. It was a very sweet kiss, our lips barely touched. I panicked and ran home.

In my diary (where I kept all my most precious secrets and dreams), I wrote the details of that moment.

This diary was a gift from my neighbor because I took care of her kids when she was working late. The diary had a lock and I carried the key with me every day. I thought my secrets were protected because of the lock. Nobody else could open it because I was the only one with access.

The next day as I returned from school, opening the door, there was my mom. Next to her was my diary, wide open…

"To live will be an awfully big adventure."

– J.M. Barrie – Peter Pan

I learned the hard way that nothing is fully protected, and anyone can break into our most sensitive and precious secrets. And there are always consequences. My mom was so devastated after reading about the kiss with Julius, for several years, that I did not date anyone.

Today, our sensitive and most precious information resides in the cyberworld, in our computer, phone, and on the Internet. We may think that the information stored in systems, accounts, or online services is kept safe. *All we need to do is use our password and nobody else can access it.* But just as I trusted that my diary was safe because it had a lock, we now know that nothing is fully protected, not even when we use passwords.

Passwords can be easily guessed by Cybermonsters if they are too simple. For example, a 7-character password consisting of lowercase letters might only take 0.29 milliseconds to crack.

According to the 2019 Verizon report, 80% of hacking-related breaches are caused because of weak and reused passwords.

Did you know that more than 23 million people use the password 123456 and that other people prefer just to use the word "password"? During the last five years, these two passwords - "123456" and "password" - have claimed the first two spots of all passwords.

Another highly popular choice for passwords are "sunshine", "iloveyou", "princess", "mynoob", "rockyou", "qwerty", "abc123", "123456789", "!@#$%^&*", "baseball" , and "hunter2" or choosing a password with a simple word that appears in sports and pop culture references.

Did you know Cybermonsters try to break your password by using an automated method entering every word in their own dictionary including English and non-English common words, spelled forward and backward, and using the most popular passwords?

Also choosing passwords with your pet's name, mother's maiden name, your kids' date of birth, spouse, or own name, can be easily guessed as some information can be found in public records or your social media accounts.

Some other methods used by Cybermonsters to crack your password are:

- Intercepting them when you transmit them through public Wi-Fi networks
- Physically stealing them if you write them down on post-it notes and place them near your computer
- Tricking you to reveal your password by pretending to be from a technical support or governmental agency or an official entity
- Observing when you type your password in public places
- Placing malware that records your keystrokes on your computer or device

Have you ever struggled to remember your password?

Have you ever written down your password only to find the paper much later and not remembering what the password was for?

Do you have a notebook containing all your passwords? Or do you send yourself coded emails or have secret notes in your phone or computer with your passwords? Or do you simply have a list with all your passwords in the cloud?

Do you use the "forgot my password" option so many times that sometimes you hate using your computer or phone?

Or do you simply not care that much about passwords?

Well, if you answered YES to any of these questions, you are not alone. It is easy to get overwhelmed as passwords are asked for in many places and often several times during the day. This is a great opportunity to use it as a powerful tool.

One way that I use the necessity of passwords is connecting my password with phrases that relate to a "Declaration", "Intention", or "Affirmation." These words are known as the fuel to manifest our goals using a mental picture.

Intentions can be used in any area of our lives, either in career, health, family, relationships, emotional, or spiritual journeys. Below is an example of how I use passwords to reinforce the message as an integral part of my life.

Examples using the intention or declaration phrase: "Every day is my best day"

Password: Ed@Y1$mB3$tD
Mix upper and lower case
Use just the initials of the word = E (every)
Include entire word "day" and replacing the a for @ = d@Y (day)
Include entire word and replacing the i for 1 and the s for an $ = 1$ (is)
Use initials of the word = m (my)
Include entire word replacing the e for 3 and s by $ (Best)
Use just the initials of the word = D (day)

I Protect what Matters most to me! 1PWM@tt3rsM2m!

Taking my business to the Top! TmyB!z2tT^p!

If you are thinking "How am I going to remember all these phrases? I'll have to write them down. What is the point of all of this if it is not helping me to simplify?"

A Password Manager becomes a very useful tool to create, manage, and monitor your passwords. When you create the master password using the power of intention, every time you need to access a particular password in the tool or log into any of your apps or system, you only need to remember one password to open the Password Manager. The tool takes care of creating unique, complex passwords for you every time.

There are several options available. When selecting a Password Manager, choose the one that offers multiple features such as:

- Warning you if you reuse or have weak passwords
- Time to change your password
- There has been a data breach
- Any of your accounts need to be changed
- A feature to change all your passwords at once.

This is very important if you become a victim of cybercrime. You can manage and reset all your accounts right away.

Password Managers offer options to store your passwords, either in the cloud or locally in your computer. Select a Password Manager that supports all your mobile devices, tablets and computers and so information can be synchronized across all of them.

A key feature of a Password Manager is to never save your master password. It is called zero knowledge protocol. That is why it is so important for you to create a phrase you will not forget. Otherwise, you are at risk of losing access to all of your accounts.

Summary

In this chapter, we have learned to put our passwords to work for us, by creating a phrase that has meaning to us, using it as an Intention, Declaration, or Affirmation. We covered the methods used by Cybermonsters to exploit our passwords and how easy it is for them to crack them. We also learned that a Password Manager will simplify our lives and that we just need to remember that one long phrase containing numbers and special characters.

Now it is your turn!

Think of your intention, affirmation or declaration. What is it that you want in your life? Write your declaration in multiple ways, find the sentence that fits best with you and start visualizing how that sentence converted as your main password can work for you.

Do not write down your password. Visualize your declaration in the form of a password and every time you type your password you tell yourself that declaration mentally.

Do an inventory of your digital life and everything that you use a password for (do not write down your passwords). For example, do you have a smart refrigerator? Do you have an account created for your car? Do you have a PIN number for your door entrance? Do you have a code set up for your phone service? List them below:

When you select a Password Manager, it will search online for all the different accounts associated with your emails. List all the email-accounts you have created in your life as this will help to change the passwords through the Password Manager tool.

Notes

What are the big takeaways for you in this chapter?

Chapter 3

K1dn@pped & @live

How do you sense danger?

Do you feel it in your belly or in your heart?

Is it an uneasy feeling that you can't put your finger on?

I was living in student housing near the university. One night, I was waiting for my boyfriend Joe to pick me up. I went out to wait on the porch of the house as he was already on his way. Standing by the porch door with my purse ready to go, I saw my co-worker Ricky driving by. He stopped and rolled down his window, "Sandra, are you okay? Did you forget your keys?"

Before I could answer Ricky's question, two individuals came out of nowhere and put a gun to each of our heads.

The gun was cold on my right temple. The man ordered me to slowly open my porch door without turning my head towards him. Then he asked me to close my eyes and not look at him. I did as he asked.

Ricky was pulled out of the driver's seat by the other man who was more agitated. We were both pushed over the backseat of the car. They pushed our heads against the seats, mostly lying down. Both men entered the car and the four of us drove away.

Their voices became more agitated. The men were discussing how and where they were going to kill us. One of them was very aggressive, while the other individual was much calmer. They continued to disagree as we kept driving for over seven hours.

Suddenly, the car stopped. Ricky and me were asked to get out of the car with our eyes closed and turn our backs toward them. I couldn't breathe. Then I heard the tires of the car spinning and they took off.

We ran and walked for several hours until we were able to get back to our families with the help of strangers.

Two months later, the police called Ricky and I. They had recovered the car. As we entered the parking lot of the police station, we saw the car covered in bullet holes. During the gunfire exchange, they had captured one individual alive.

The man was in a line-up and the police promised he couldn't see us through the small glass windows.

"You must try to identify him from the robbery. Was this the man that pointed the gun at you?"

I was speechless. Then the police chief entered the room and asked me, "Kiddo, why are you alive?" I couldn't articulate any words.

The Chief said, "Look, the two individuals who kidnapped both of you and took the car were part of an organized crime gang focused on robbing armored vehicles. They needed the car as they were going to rob an armored vehicle the next day. Having done these robberies in multiple cities, they have never left anyone alive. Wow, you really have a guardian angel."

I never found the answer to that question, "Why are you alive?" After a while, it didn't matter anymore. I was alive, and had dreams and promises to fulfill.

---

*"I won't run, I will stand and look ahead to what I must do,
I must face the fear, I won't let it control me anymore."*
— *Gray Fullbuster – Fairy-Tail*

There are blurry lines between our physical and cyber safety; both are equally important. Sometimes we can't see the danger of waiting on our doorstep, as was my case, when I was kidnapped from a place I considered "safe."

Today, Cybermonsters can be anywhere, visible or invisible, behind a keyboard.

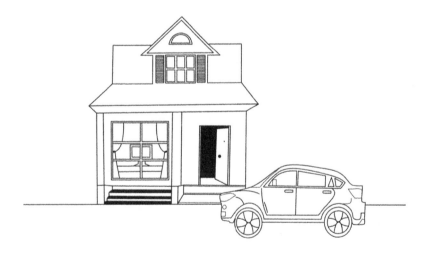

When we post on social media where we are, who we are with, or simply that we are home alone, we are giving away precious information that could compromise our family's safety or our own.

Sharing pictures of our house or having location services enabled on our phones or on our social media profiles means we are also giving away our geolocation that can be easily translated into our address.

Next time you are eager to post that you are going on vacation, think again, and perhaps share those memories after you return. If you have pictures of your home on social media channels, there is an option for you to delete the previous history location and turn off your location for future posts.

The *Happily Ever Cyber!* book series includes: "protecting your social media accounts" and "protecting your computer, phone, and other devices." These books cover the details of how you can remove location services, how to improve the security of your devices, and how to protect yourself, your family, your business, and everything that matters to you.

1s @nything Re@lly Free?

When you were a kid, did your mom or dad ever tell you to never accept a gift from a stranger or never to trust people you don't know?

During our honeymoon cruise, my husband Ricardo and I made a stop at one of the Caribbean Islands. We decided to explore it on our own instead of taking a tour.

The day was beautiful and sunny with a deep blue sky. The ocean was all around us and the breeze was refreshing. We felt so in love with each other.

As we kept walking, two men were approaching,

"Hey guys, welcome to our island."

As we went to return their greeting, one of the men right away placed a bead bracelet on my left hand, while the other man blocked our way.

The man blocking our way opened his hand and offered us a variety of drugs. Immediately, I took off the bracelet and gave it back. We politely rejected the offer and walked away.

They were no longer friendly.

"Peter did not feel very brave; indeed, he felt he was going to be sick. But that made no difference to what he had to do."
— C.S. Lewis, The Chronicles of Narnia

Every time I see a free offer in a flyer, email, an application (app), or in a browser, I remember that day at the beach learning the meaning of "free." Free could mean *we* are the product. Everything always has a price tag, whether we see it or not.

However, not all freely given offers are motivated by bad intentions. Today, many marketers and business owners share their free services to gain your trust and earn your business.

Below we will explore three scenarios for free online offers. The choice is always yours.

- An upfront gift or offer
- A hidden price
- A trap

We might not know the consequences of accepting something "free" until much later, so let's explore what each option means.

An upfront gift or offer

In this case, there is an exchange of information. For example, when we visit a website, we are frequently asked to provide our email address, name, and/or phone number. If the item has value to us, we choose to give our information. In essence, it is a trade and each participant gets something in return.

If you receive emails for services or websites you have never visited or subscribed, move those messages to the spam or junk folder;

be aware that unsubscribing from these emails could provide a validation that your email is real.

A hidden price

After my diary incident when my mom read all my secrets and dreams, she started following me around.

She was like the Droopy cartoon, the small dog that appeared everywhere, every time. I really liked this cartoon, except when the cartoon became my reality. Every time I turned around, my mom was there. Sometimes she showed up in plain sight in front of my school, church, or at my volleyball practices. Other times she was hidden and observing all my moves. "Come on, mom!"

Today, if my mom wanted to check on me, she could have stayed home and still tracked all my moves. That is, if I were carrying a cellphone, because there are many different apps and location services available that anyone can use to know where you are.

There are good reasons for these services. Parents today might enable location services on their kids' phones to protect them and to know where they are while they are at work, traveling, or for many other reasons. In my mom's case, she wanted to protect me. She feared I would get pregnant as young as she did, and that would prevent me from achieving my dreams.

Location services are useful services when we want to know the weather in the place we are or to use our GPS for directions. In these situations, using our geolocation might be appropriate, but what about the times that we don't even know we are being tracked?

Do you ever read the privacy notices or legal terms when you download a free app or buy a new service?

Most people choose not to read privacy statements because they are long and full of legal jargon. We scroll down to the end and click "I accept" without knowing what terms we are accepting and what we are giving away for that "free" app we want.

Many free apps request that location services are enabled when we are installing the app or to send notifications to us. These features, most of the time, are not needed for the app to function. If they are needed, you could limit its use only while you are using the app.

Many apps collect our information including the phone number, the serial number of our device, our email, name, date of birth, etc. In some cases, these apps share or could sell our information to third party companies that are interested in knowing exactly where, when, and how long we visit specific places or want to have access to our data.

When you decide to download a free app rather than downloading the paid-version (which can range from $0.99 to $9.99), please ask yourself if paying with your own personal information is really worth it.

Privacy topics are becoming more prevalent as different regulations are in place or in progress to be implemented. But what is privacy? Why should privacy matter to us?

Privacy is a person's right to control who, how, and who can access their personal information. When my mom opened and read my diary, she breached my personal space. However, "moms are just moms" trying to protect us in the best way they know at the time. We need to watch out for Cybermonsters or other services that could use our privacy for their gain.

Next time you download a new app, check out their privacy notice or policy and focus on the sections that detail what and how your information is shared, scroll down and at least skim the document. If you read that they sell, trade or transfer your information to third parties and that by using the app you are providing consent, it means you have no control over what they do with your information. When you are aware of how the information collected about you is being used and shared, you are empowered to make the right choice about whether to install the app or not.

Most apps today allow you to customize the privacy settings and limit how much information is collected about you or at least how much analytics can be shared with the app vendor. Please check the settings of your location services and know which apps can track your steps and turn off the ones that don't require this information to function.

A trap

When you are online, activate your inner instincts and ask yourself: What does this service or person really want from me? Do I know them? What am I trading off?

When the offer seems too good to be true, most of the time it is probably not true at all. Do me a favor, just walk away!

Did you know that when you use the Internet there is a record stored in your computer with all the sites you have visited?

Did you know that your online behavior is visible to your Internet provider (ISPs) and that they may record details of your Internet usage in accordance with legal requirements or country regulations?

Do you ever wonder why and how you suddenly start receiving ads and promotions about sport shoes or new cars that you just happened to search for online a few hours ago?

A computer "cookie" is a tiny file placed inside a website and then dropped and stored in your computer when you visit that website. Cookies report your online habits, what sites you visit, your demographics, when you leave items in a shopping cart at an online retailer, etc.

There are many different types of cookies. A common one is called the "preference-cookie," which saves information you have entered on the website so next time you visit the same site it recognizes you. Many retailers and online businesses rely on cookies for their marketing and advertising efforts.

One piece of good news is that cookies are stored on your mobile devices or tablets only as a web view to display your online content. This information cannot be shared between the apps you have installed on your device. Cookies have a limited lifespan that can range from a single session to several months, although some "persistent-cookies" can be stored much longer.

Private browsing is a feature available on your phone, devices and computer. When you perform a search on the Internet, it protects you from people snooping at your browsing history. When you use the "private window" or the "incognito window," your browser does not store cookies, does not save your username and password, or store your browsing history. This feature is very useful, especially when visiting websites where you process sensitive transactions, such as online banking, online purchases, filing your taxes, etc. Using private browsing is as easy as tapping on your phone browser or selecting the incognito or private window. More details for how to use private browsing are shared in my book "How To Protect Your Computer, Phone and Other Electronic Devices," (which is book 2 of the *Happily Ever Cyber!* series).

Privacy concerns and regulations are becoming more prevalent. You may have seen many emails asking you to accept the new terms and conditions of the service, or accept the privacy notices, or to confirm the service can send you email communications.

You may have also seen that when visiting certain websites, many will ask the visitor to acknowledge and/or accept the use of cookies. This is done in compliance with laws and regulations some countries are required to create in order to protect consumers.

What else happens in the online world when we navigate the Internet ocean?

As cybercrime evolves, Cybermonsters find other ways to infect your devices that don't require you to click or download anything online. One of these creative cyber-attacks is Malvertising. Let's review how it works.

Malvertising

The word Malvertising is a combination of Malware and Advertising. It refers to the practice of infecting ads in websites to spread malware to your computer or mobile devices. Malvertising could appear as abrupt alerts, tickling offers, banners, or pop-up ads.

Cybermonsters buy ad space on trustworthy websites which appear to us as legitimate ads, but they have hidden code inside them that could redirect you to their malicious website, or simply install the malware right away on your computer or devices instantly.

In some cases, you don't even have to click the ad. By just hovering your mouse over the ad, it triggers the malware to be installed in your computer. In other cases, clicking the X to close the pop-up window or simply loading the page with the infected ad on it are other ways to distribute the malware. Malvertising could also affect large company websites.

Malvertising and adware are sometimes confused because they both use advertising to distribute the malware, but they are different. Malvertising is a code embedded in the ad that you may get after visiting a particular website, while adware is a program that runs in your computer, constantly displaying ads in your device, and disrupting your browsing experience.

Malvertising activity is higher during weekends and holiday shopping season because people are actively looking for discounts. They are more prone to click on the "amazing deal" or coupon ad.

There are two main types of Malvertising: Drive-by-Downloads and Click to Download.

Drive-by-Downloads

Refers to an unintentional download of malware or malicious software onto your computer or mobile devices that makes you vulnerable to a cyber-attack. You don't have to click or press "download" to become infected.

This type of attack uses small pieces of code and is not very sophisticated. Cybermonsters install this unnoticed program which gives them access to your computer or mobile device to install additional malware.

You could be infected when checking your favorite news website. If the site has the malicious code, it will start scanning your computer to find security vulnerabilities and open holes in your operating system, Internet browsers, software, or apps of any kind that have not been updated.

Click to Download

You must interact with an ad for the infection of your computer to occur. The ads imitate real ads in order to deceive you, enticing you to click.

There are many things we can do to reduce the chances of getting infected by Malvertising. For example, save the website URLs for the most sensitive sites you use (such as your bank's) into your browser favorites folder so it takes you directly to the website.

Notice when you do an online search that the first results include an "Ad version" and a few lines below you can see the regular website without ads. Create the habit of not clicking the ad websites. If you are interested in a particular ad, do a separate search for the company or product. The same deal should be offered on their website if the offer is legit.

Summary

In this chapter, we have covered the importance of physical security and protecting our location services when we use our phones and social media platforms.

Additionally, we navigated the meaning of getting something for "free" and the choices we all must make to keep our information private and safe. It is helpful to understand that Cybermonsters continue to find creative ways to get to us and that clicking is not necessarily the only way to be infected. We still need to be vigilant... and we need to develop our sixth sense online!

In the next chapter, we will explore why a plan and a self-assessment are the first steps on our cyber ride to protect what matters most to us.

Now it is your turn!

Think of a moment in which you shared something you now wish you would not have shared on social media or online. What happened? How did you feel?

Describe how your information could be compromised. How would you react to it? What would you do?

What was the last post that you shared online that made you very happy?

Notes

What are the big takeaways for you in this chapter?

Chapter 4

Pract!cing $afe Cyber R1des

D° you remember the first time you rode a bike?

Where were you? How old were you?

Who was holding the bike for you to get going and start pedaling? How did you feel?

It was a beautiful spring day to be in the park. The blue sky was magnificent. The cold breeze was offset by the warmth of the sun, making it very comfortable.

I was trying to get on my bike… trying, because balance has never been my strength. My feet were on the ground and the saddle was tall. Holding on to the handlebars, he says, "Are you ready, honey?"

"Yes, I am ready."

"Do not worry. I will hold the back of your bike and won't let go until you are pedaling. You've got this."

I click my left foot on the pedal. My right leg is supporting my body, so I do not fall off. One, two, three, and my right foot goes off the ground onto the pedal. I am wobbling and wobbling but I know he is holding my bike and that I will not fall off.

I start pedaling, yes, pedaling. He is running holding the bike while I am pedaling and still wobbling, and then he lets go of me. I am pedaling a bicycle.

My dream had just come true. I am riding my own new bike. Uh oh... focus. And bam... I am on the ground... ouch.

"Can we try this again, honey?" I say, to my husband Ricardo.

Yes, that is right. I was in my 30s and my husband was holding my bike and teaching me how to ride. I chose to use a clipless pedal which is a small pedal with a locking mechanism that attaches directly to your bike shoes. The shoes clip into the pedal meaning your whole leg is connected to your bike. I wanted to become a real cyclist.

There is a girl in my office whose name is Andy. She is very athletic. Andy is a runner and a cyclist. When she walks into a meeting room, Andy lights up the room with her presence and joyful personality. One day when we were in a meeting, Andy asked me if I would join her on a bike ride that she just signed up for.

"You have to do this with me. We will have a blast together. A small group from the office will do it… come on, girl, let's do it!"

And one more time I said, "Yes, I can do this."

RAGBRAI is a bike ride across Iowa and is the oldest, longest, and largest recreational bicycle ride in the world. It is close to 500 miles for seven days. The event includes over 10,000 riders + additional riders in charge of the logistics and vendors. It is a massive event.

We were four months away from RAGBRAI. And again, I said "yes" without thinking about how I would do it.

This was my opportunity to get to know Andy better and to take on a challenge, as my cycling expertise went as far as learning the basics.

After I got my new road bike and all the equipment I needed, my next challenge was to complete the first group ride.

For the last two weeks, I had been practicing and practicing. Finally, I had gained balance on the bike, at least most of the time. Nothing was broken yet, despite the many times I had fallen off. I was excited to be with the group and share the RAGBRAI experience.

We all met on a Saturday morning. There are seven of us going on this ride. I did not know everyone. Andy was there, Brian, Paula and her husband Gary, John, and Greg, who is the fastest rider. We were ready to go.

Everyone started pedaling. I didn't have a good start. My shoe wouldn't click on the pedal. My heart was pounding, and I was sweating. "Come on, I am not even riding yet."

Finally, I took off, but everyone was already ahead of me. I was riding as fast as I could, but I could not catch up to them. "They are going so fast - or am I going too slow?"

My heart rate seemed to be so high. It felt like my chest was going to explode. I was out of air. I still didn't have a heart rate monitor; I thought, I should get that.

I was grateful there were many red lights and that they waited for me. I was finally with the group.

"Oh no" - now we must cross a busy street - and there were so many cars. I am not confident in taking off on the bicycle. I still wobbled a lot and my clipless shoe was not helping. I waited until no more cars were around or behind me. Again, I was left behind.

I tried to catch up to them. This continued for the next two hours. I was exhausted. We did approximately an 18-mile ride. I quickly realized the need to buy a bike computer, an essential tool for a cyclist.

"What the heck am I going to do in the RAGBRAI? I am not going to make it!"

After the ride, we were at a coffee shop. Gary approached me and said, "Hey Sandra, you might want to consider getting a coach. I know a guy if you are interested."

And without thinking about it, I said, "YES. Let's go see him."

Have you ever been challenged by a friend?

What if you don't have the skills and knowledge to do it?

Would you choose not to try it?

Would you seek help from an expert?

Jay has a fitness studio and trains triathletes and cyclists. He is in great shape. I told Jay that I signed up for RAGBRAI and that I didn't have much experience cycling, but I was willing to listen, take his direction, and do the work every day.

Jay explained that he certainly could create a detailed plan for me to follow and prepare for my ride. I said, "Yes, Jay. Can we start now?"

Jay replied immediately, "Sandra, first I need to know your fitness level. Then I can provide you with recommendations that you can follow, based on your physical capabilities, while also considering what is needed for a ride like RAGBRAI. An assessment is critical to build your skills to make cycling simple so it can become second nature to you."

I said "yes" to the assessment and training. "I've got this."

The next day, I went to my two-hour physical assessment in Jay's studio. He measured my cardiovascular strength, had me run and jump everywhere. Using different tools Jay measured how flexible I was. He tested my balance. I couldn't close my eyes and stand on one foot. Neither was I able to walk a straight line with my eyes closed. I now know why it is so hard to keep my balance on the bike. I was born without this capability.

Jay also made me pedal a trainer bike hooked up to a computer to measure my pedal stroke, my power, my heart rate, and other cycling measures with terms I had no idea existed. In the first five minutes, I wanted to quit and forget about RAGBRAI. Then I thought of my promise - I am not a quitter.

The assessment test showed that I clearly had a long way to go, but instead of being discouraged, I was excited to know someone was guiding me. Jay was creating a map for me to follow with a series of recommendations to build and improve my cardiovascular strength, my core, and overall endurance and flexibility. I needed to have balance and power on the bike, and even learn how to drink water and eat while I was still pedaling.

Jay created a detailed plan for me to cover the basics of cycling and gave me specific instructions on how to train including the best practices to follow to get in shape and ready for RAGBRAI.

I followed Jay's plan "to a T" and practiced every single day. It was scary, hard, and many times I doubted myself, but I kept going and learned and prepared for my 500-mile ride.

Part of my plan included practicing what to do in case of an accident and how to react if that happened. After four months of training, I was in great shape. I completed over 2,500 miles preparing for the biggest cycling adventure of my life.

During RAGBRAI, I was able to keep up with everyone, even with Greg. And that week, when unexpected situations happened, like almost crashing into two other cyclists and falling down, getting lost many times and taking the wrong path that added more miles to my ride without having enough water or food, I was still able to manage all the unpredicted events. Why? Because of my training, preparation, and the skills I developed when I followed Jay's recommendations.

Yes, I did a century ride (which is 100 miles, about 35 extra miles than what we needed to do for the day) - believe me it was not part of my plan.

I finished RAGBRAI. Dipping the tires of my bike in the Mississippi River was a great moment of joy.

"Dreams do come true, if only we wish hard enough. You can have anything in life if you will sacrifice everything else for it."

– J.M Barrie – Peter Pan

At the beginning of my cycling journey, I didn't know the basics or the skills to take on this ride. There were many things that could have happened to me or others around me, from breaking a bone to getting killed or causing an accident, and risking someone else's life. None of this happened because I reached out to someone with the skills and expertise based on prior experience. Someone who understood the basics and was able to assess, teach, and provide me with recommendations considering my level of expertise and physical condition.

When I followed Jay's recommendations that were simple, to the point, and pragmatic, I developed the skills needed and cycling then became second nature.

Knowing how to ride does not mean I am done with training, conditioning, and learning. There are external forces; the winter, road changes, our health, or any other situations that arise so we cyclists need to continually keep up our training to enjoy the ride.

Cybersecurity is very much like cycling. At the beginning, it may seem impossible to learn the terminology, learn the basics of the technology, and take action to protect our devices, our data, and our cyber life. There is a lot that could happen when we ride the cyber world, Cybermonsters could steal our identity and impersonate us, they could have access to our personal information, our business, our personal finances, and our family.

You can take action to minimize the risk of this happening by self-assessing your skills, following the plan to build your cyber muscles, and implementing the recommendations from the *Happily Ever Cyber!* book series.

Like cycling, we are never done with training and learning in cybersecurity. On the cyber ride we are always trying to catch up to the latest data breaches, trends in technology, or ways Cybermonsters will try to get to us. We must continually learn how to protect our personal information, finances, data, family and everything else that truly matters to us.

Summary

In this chapter, we have learned that reaching out to someone with the skills and expertise necessary to guide us is essential to learn the fundamentals to protect your personal information, your family, your business, and your data, and protect what matters most to you.

When was the last time you did a self-assessment?

After you completed the assessment, did you have a list of recommendations to help you?

Are you ready for your cyber self-assessment?

Notes

What are the big takeaways for you in this chapter?

Chapter 5

D F@iry G0dm0ther Pl@n

"Even miracles take a little time."

— The Fairy Godmother

Strengthen Your Password

Backup Your Information

Protect Your Geolocation

Yes, there are many simple recommendations and practices we can incorporate into our daily lives to protect ourselves, our families, our data, and all that matters to us. As mentioned before, it takes constant learning because the threats change every day and Cybermonsters are always looking for new ways to get us.

A self-assessment helps us identify the areas that we want to improve upon. It provides us with insights about the practices we need to implement in our daily lives or simply identify what we want to focus on to develop our new skills.

This cyber assessment is a simple tool that provides you the basics that are covered in the next books of the *Happily Ever Cyber!* series. They represent a sampling of what basic actions we need to focus on to reduce the chances of becoming a victim of cybercrime or identity theft.

The rest of the books in the *Happily Ever Cyber!* series are all about the *How*. We have broken down the topics into individual books so you can decide to protect what matters most to you.

The next six books of the *Happily Ever Cyber!* series are:

Book 2:

How To Protect Your Computer & Phone Against Hackers, Scammers and Cybermonsters

Book 3:

How To Protect Your Email Against Hackers, Scammers and Cybermonsters

Book 4:

How To Protect Yourself While Traveling Against Hackers, Scammers and Cybermonsters

Book 5:

How To Protect Your Passwords Against Hackers, Scammers and Cybermonsters

Book 6:

How To Protect Your Identity Against Hackers, Scammers and Cybermonsters

Book 7:

How To Protect Your Social Media Against Hackers, Scammers and Cybermonsters

In the cyber assessment there are four sample questions from each of the books in the *Happily Ever Cyber!* series that can be answered in three different ways:

Yes, always

When you answer a question with "Yes, always", it means that you do these practices without even thinking of them, that they are integrated in your daily routine. This is the way to ensure your data, your family, and you are protected.

I know how, but I don't do it

You have heard of best practices for cybersecurity and you even know how to execute them. But you don't do them, you don't have the time, or you have not incorporated them into your daily habits.

I need help

We do not have to explain this one. You need help and I am here for you. In the other books in the *Happily Ever Cyber!* series, each of the cyber assessment topics are covered (further details on the content are part of our journey together). Remember that I've got your hand.

Let's complete the next simple cyber self-assessment by checking each question with the answer that is closest to your reality. There are no scores, right, or wrong. The intention is just for you to know at a high level the basic principles you are currently doing, the ones that you know how but don't do them, and the ones you need help with.

If you score "Yes, always" to each of the questions, move on to the next phase by asking yourself these questions from the perspective of your family, your employees, or those around you that you want to protect.

I am excited for you to complete the self-assessment tool. When I went through my cycling assessment, the value for me was knowing the areas I needed to focus on, which allowed me to have a plan to learn the basics of cycling until it became second nature to me and I could enjoy the ride.

Use this tool to guide you and to encourage you to embark on our cyber ride together. If you do not know how to respond to some of these questions, do not worry! we are going to cover all of them. The importance of the self-assessment is that you are making the choice. When we decide to protect what matters most to us, we are reducing the chances of becoming a victim of cybercrime or identity theft.

You can complete the information in the next pages. Additionally, you have the option to complete the assessment online at HowICyber.com and you can review your score and recommendations for the next steps to follow.

Your Simple Cyber Self-Assessment ©

Sample questions	😃 Yes, always	😕 I know how, but I don't do it	😣 I need help!
Protecting your Computer, Phone, and Devices			
Do you review what apps in your mobile devices are using location services and can track where you are?			
Do you update your systems and apps on your computer, phone, and devices to keep Cybermonsters away?			
Do you use an administrator or master account to go online, check emails, and do all your daily tasks?			
Do you regularly back-up your computer, phone, and devices to prevent losing your information?			
Protecting Your Email from Ransomware			
Do you know how to recognize phishing emails to avoid ransomware?			
Do you validate if a link is safe before clicking on it?			
Do you check if attachments are safe before opening them?			
Do you know how to share sensitive and personal information securely?			

Sample questions	😀 Yes, always	😐 I know how, but I don't do it	😣 I need help!
Protecting Yourself While Traveling			
Do you know how to protect your phone data if using a public smart charger?			
Do you know the dangers of public devices and how to protect yourself?			
Do you know how to secure your data when traveling?			
Do you disable your connectivity services when traveling?			
Protecting Your Passwords			
Do you use a different password for each of your accounts?			
Do you make your passwords work for you?			
Do you use an extra layer of protection for your most sensitive and important accounts?			
When you buy new technology or equipment, do you change the manufacturing passwords before the first use?			

Sample questions from the book series	Yes, always	I know how, but I don't do it	I need help!
Protecting Yourself from Identity Theft			
Do you know how to protect your credit score so Cybermonsters cannot open a credit line or accounts impersonating you?			
Do you have alerts in place to let you know if someone is impersonating you?			
Do you know if you have been a victim of cyber-crime?			
Do you know what to do in case your identity has been taken by Cybermonsters?			
Protecting Your Online Presence			
Have you protected your social media accounts so Cybermonsters cannot steal your information?			
Do you know how to recognize if a website is unsafe?			
Have you removed location services from your social media pictures so Cybermonsters or others cannot find where you live?			
Do you use private browsing when searching online?			

Summary

In this chapter, we learned that a self-assessment of our current state is very important to achieve our goal of protecting what matters most. When we have a clear direction of where to focus, and follow expert recommendations, we can really make progress in our journey of learning how to live *Happily Ever Cyber!*

Cybersecurity like cycling, scuba diving, or learning any new skill or sport could feel overwhelming, scary. At times, we might doubt ourselves and want to give up. We have learned that there are many different things that could happen to us or others around us.

Yet, what is the alternative?

Would you choose not to take any action and just wait for Cybermonsters to get your personal information, steal your money, or impersonate you to conduct illegal activities on your behalf or simply endanger your family?

The more we cover the basics and fundamentals of making cybersecurity simple and protecting what matters to us, the more we get to enjoy this cyber ride.

Choosing to change the perception of the cyber world we live in is essential, and I am counting on you because once we make the choice then cybersecurity can become second nature and simply be part of our lives.

We are on this ride together to live *Happily Ever Cyber!*

Now it is your turn!

Look at your assessment and select three questions you care the most about under the "I need help" or the "I know how, but I don't do it" columns and list them below.

Now, list five things that you care the most about to protect (i.e. your bank account, your computer, your family, your identity, particular data, and other precious information.) After you write them down, return to chapter one and compare your answers. Has anything changed? If yes, ask yourself why and write it down.

Notes

What are the big takeaways for you in this chapter?

Chapter 6

Us!ng Checkl!t 2b $@f3

When Jay walked me through my assessment, he also gave me a checklist with basic information about cycling, some of the tools I should consider, what kind of clothes, how I should dress properly for cycling and some daily, weekly and monthly routines I should incorporate as part of my plan. I didn't know most of the terminology and that was okay. As I started with my program, I was eventually able to understand what those initial things in my cycling journey meant.

Checklists are a great way to keep us on track and ensure we don't forget things. They are especially useful when we must do repetitive tasks.

The checklist below is a simple and direct way for you to start taking action about the basics of cybersecurity. Don't stress if you are not clear on how to do them because that is what we will cover in more detail in each of the books in the *Happily Ever Cyber!* series and the supplemental content in our social media channels @Way2Protect.

"It is not in doing what you like, but in liking what you do that is the secret of happiness."

— J.M. Barrie – Peter Pan

Checklist - How to Protect yourself Against Hackers, Scammers and Cybermonsters

Protecting your Computer, Phone, and Devices	
Validate Apps using location services and remove those that don't require it to function	
Update the software on your electronic devices:	
On your computer	
On your phone	

Other devices (smart watch, tablet)	
Update the Apps on your electronic devices:	
On your computer	
On your phone	
Other devices (smart watch, tablet)	
Update your browser	
Use a regular account to go online, check emails, and do all your normal tasks	
Change the password of your administrator account and only use it when you require to update or install new software on your computer	
Schedule a regular back-up to prevent losing your information	
On your computer	
On your phone	
Other devices (smart watch, tablet)	
Protecting Your Email from Ransomware	
Validate if a link is safe before clicking on it	
Check attachments are safe before opening them	
Validate your email settings to classify spam	
Install an anti-virus/anti-malware that scans your email attachments and links	
Protecting Yourself While Traveling	
Pack your own phone charger	
Change your phone settings to not connect to public Wi-Fi by default	
Disable Wi-Fi and Bluetooth when traveling	
When handing your credit card and personal ID don't give them at the same time	
Protecting Your Passwords	

Install a Password Manager	
Create a master password that inspires or motivates you every day	
Create a different password for each of your accounts	
Activate an extra layer of protection for your most sensitive and important accounts	
Change the manufacturing passwords of your home network devices	
Protecting Yourself from Identity Theft	
Create an inventory of your accounts	
Create alerts to let you know if you are being impersonated	
Check your email in HaveIbeenPwned website and if your account has been compromised change your password	
Place a freeze on your credit score	
Use one separate email for your sensitive transactions	
Protecting Your Online Presence	
Update the security and privacy setting in your Social Media accounts	
Bookmark the most important websites you visit	
Remove location services from your social media pictures	
Use private browsing while searching online	

Summary

This chapter gives you a tool you can use to start taking control of your cyber ride and taking care of the basics. Some of the items in the checklist are actions you can take care of right away while others will require more details on how to do them.

No worries, I am here holding your hand. We are going to incorporate these practices in the checklist as part of your routine, but we will do it in a way that is not overwhelming or going to paralyze you.

Our goal is for you to protect what matters most to you while still enjoying your cyber world. Now take a deep breath and remember this is how we all can live *Happily Ever Cyber!*

Now it is your turn!

From the checklist select three items that impacted you the most. Do not worry if you don't know how to execute them, just write down what surprised you the most and why.

Look at the checklist and select three things you can take care of within the next twenty-four hours and commit to doing them!

Notes

What are the big takeaways for you in this chapter?

Chapter 7

---··──···──

Y0ur Cy8er $t0r!es!

This section includes a set of real-life stories of cybercrime and identity theft. The purpose is not to scare you, but to encourage and inspire you to take control of your cyber world. Some authors have opted to remain anonymous, and we respected their privacy.

When we go through the vulnerability of our identities being stolen or as a victim of cybercrime, it could be very hard to trust again. You may prefer to pretend it didn't happen to avoid reliving the pain, or you may prefer nobody to know that Cybermonsters impacted your life.

I am very grateful for each of these leaders sharing what happened in their stories and what they learned from their painful experiences. Thank you for your bravery - you are helping many others protect their data, their families and their businesses from hackers, scammers, and Cybermonsters.

These stories could have happened to anyone: to you, to someone in your family or in your business. After you read the stories, please take a few minutes to reflect on them and make a commitment to put in place the three recommendations that I've added at the end of each story. These will help you live *Happily Ever Cyber!*

If you have a cyber story that you would like to share with us to be featured in the *Happily Ever Cyber!* series, please contact us at https://sandraestok.com/contact/

"Peter did not feel very brave; indeed, he felt he was going to be sick. But that made no difference to what he had to do."
— C.S. Lewis - The Chronicles of Narnia

Identity theft can happen more than once!

Tim

I'm in Oregon, and someone in Georgia used my name and Social Security number (SSN), but they used it to open up a gas account for their apartment. I don't know how they got my SSN.

This person had moved to several different apartments in Georgia and used my name and SSN each time and never paid the bills. I would have never known about it had I not looked at my credit report and saw all of these charges since 2017. Those had made it into collections and then I had to contact them and dispute them on the credit report. The collections agency still said, "this is you." I've never stepped foot in Georgia, I've never even been there.

Long story short, it took almost 6 months to get it all the way cleared up. It wasn't much money; I think they were counting on the fact that I would pay it just to get it out from my name rather than fight it. I told myself, "I'm not going to take responsibility for it," because then if I take responsibility for this, then what's next, will they start buying houses, cars, what else can happen in Georgia under my name?

I'm a psychiatric mental health nurse practitioner. As a provider, we are on insurance panels, to be able to bill and save payment, even if you're working for another organization, you're still on this insurance panel. One of those insurance companies had a data breach, they didn't know how much information was accessed, but basically all of the therapists in my organization also had their data breached.

There was also some kind of phishing scam, where someone opened an email, and it downloaded a virus, it held the computers hostage, some sort of ransomware. Luckily, they caught it fairly quickly but even so, they had to send out letters to all of the clients who were served by the organization from 10 or 15 years back, saying "your data may have been breached."

I put the fraud alert on each of the credit bureaus.

Months later, my payroll department received an email using my name but from a different email address saying, "can I change what institution I use for my direct deposit?" And, thankfully, they emailed back to that person but also copied my work email. I responded immediately, this is not my personal email address, do not change my financial institution.

I'm glad for all the checkpoints and processes in place that prevented someone taking my paycheck, without doing the work!

Summary

Our identities are very personal and when someone steals our document IDs, health records, our passports, financial information, and any other similar document that validates our existence in society, we could feel overwhelmed by the loss and the pain we must endure to restore it.

When our SSN is stolen, additional scams could also happen. One common scam occurs when you receive emails, mail, and phone calls from Cybermonsters pretending to be from the IRS (Internal Revenue Services), or when they solicit W-2 forms information from human resource professionals, or by requesting changes in your payroll account. Cybermonsters pretend to be you in order to have access to what you have.

Tim's story shows us that sometimes we have no idea how our information was stolen, but once it is exposed, we could be impersonated in many different ways. He took the necessary steps to restore his information and didn't give up until his record was clean, choosing not to live in a state of fear, instead be proactive and take the necessary actions to protect your information and your family from hackers, scammers, and Cybermonsters to live *Happily Ever Cyber!*

There are many things you can do once your SSN has been compromised to protect your information.

Consider these three recommendations:

1. Place a freeze on your credit report with each of the credit bureaus (Equifax, Experian, and TransUnion) so nobody

can open a new account or credit card under your name. This is a free service and you can lift the freeze when needed. This does not affect your credit score. Consider placing a fraud alert if you are a recent victim of identity theft.

2. Frequently check your credit report, your social security account, bank statements and create alerts to monitor your name online.

3. Stay aware! pay careful attention to emails with links and attachments and consider shredding all your paper documents that contain personal or business sensitive information.

If you or someone you know has become a victim of identity theft, report it to the IdentityTheft.gov and report the theft of your Social Security to the IRS to the Identity Protection to prevent tax fraud.

One simple click turned into a nightmare!

Vicky L.

I hired a great web development team and they created this incredible website for me. About four months into it, we were launching the website in Spanish. Someone on my team opened a comment sent to us through the website. It was opened, and we didn't think twice about it, it looked like spam, which we get all the time.

Three days later, my social media team went in to take a graphic from my website, and they realized we're being re-routed to an adult website.

Some of the images were very demeaning to women, which is an issue because I deal with financial empowerment for women. Our message always has to be one of positivity, of empowerment, of the future is female. "I am worthy," is our tagline, and this reroute was very embarrassing.

I was out doing media for my book, and telling people to go to my website, and instead of them seeing what I wanted them to see, they were seeing deplorable content.

When I got on the phone with my website developer, he said "we're going to get to it, but it may not be quickly."

I freaked out and I am thinking I need to get this off here now, not Monday. Even though that's a reasonable timeline, a lot of people visit my website when they're relaxing at home.

I bought software online to figure out what is happening on my website. They weren't cheap, they were a couple hundred dollars. Some of these products were not effective, but as I was in panic to figure out how to fix this problem, I kept trying until one of the products I purchased provided me with the confirmation: "You got malware on your website."

We spend countless hours of work to get rid of the offending redirect, get back online, and to recreate the changes we had made previously to the website because we didn't have a recent backup.

Not only did this cost me money, it cost me time, and it also cost me reputation risk. I lost the opportunity to grow my mailing list (prospective customers), which is money to an entrepreneur. At least 5,000 people would've signed up to be on my list as I had a media tour in the west coast of Florida none of that happened.

I had to reach out to TV producers, editors, and PR people who had been working on the media campaign to explain we had a technical problem. My biggest worry was, what if they visited my website and I was spreading malware to my customers or prospects? It's a reputation risk that to this day I worry about.

I feel very lucky. It could've been a lot worse if our customers' sensitive data was impacted, but it didn't affect them. I just wish I knew at the time how careful we had to be with getting spam on what is just a contact form on our website. Now I check the website numerous times a day, and I've changed my processes. This situation was a lot, I had never experienced anything like that. Ever!

Summary

Research [14] indicates that over 30,000 websites are hacked every day. There is a misconception that websites are safe because they don't contain sensitive information; however, the reality is that Cybermonsters infect websites as they could easily spread more malware to your website visitors.

As Vicky indicated, this was one of her major concerns because it is not only detrimental to your company brand and reputation, but it could also impact your SEO ranking (Search Engine Optimization) meaning your website could be negatively impacted on search results.

Consider these three recommendations:

1. Keep your website software updated. Including all the plugins and additional tools used.
2. Backup your site regularly.
3. Setup a Google Webmaster email alert so they can alert if your website is being attacked by malware or your pages are not indexed.

Report related Internet crimes or fake websites to the *FBI Crime Complaint Center (IC3.gov)* because your story can help track patterns of fraud and contribute to stopping Cybermonsters.

What? My card was sold online!

Michelle Mras

I'm a military spouse. I went to an office supply store to get supplies for my business. When I got there, the clerk said that their computer system was down today, and she asked, "Can I take an impression of your card?" I asked what that was, and she told me it was the old school way where they rub it to get the numbers on the card. I said, "Oh! Okay."

The employee did that rubbing of my card, she packed up my supplies, and I walked out the door. I hadn't gotten maybe 20 yards away from the store, when I got a call from my bank, asking, "Are you in Paris right now?" I said, "No, I'm not in Paris, I'm in Colorado Springs," and they replied "Well, you just made a very large purchase. In Paris. Oh, and now you're in Germany."

The woman from the bank told me my card was sold online, and I thought, "What do you mean by sold it online?" Maybe they have my husband's card, my husband is deployed. She read me my card number and asked me if it was mine. "Yes, it is!"

I had just left the office supply store. It was just so shocking to me how quickly it was sold. And the only way it could have been done was by that person who worked in the office supply store.

I was struggling, do I go back in there and grab that girl by the neck and say, "you stole my card," or do I just let the bank handle the situation? I could still see her through the glass of the office supply store - she didn't even leave the front desk; how did she steal my card so quickly?

The purchases were all being done online. The bank couldn't stop any of them because it was going faster than the machine could stop them. They could flag my account as these were not my purchases. Within the hour, my checking account, since that was the account I used, was negative $30,000 within the first hour, by the end of the day it was over $100,000.

It was astronomical how fast they were spending my money, or my lack of money at that point, and how fast it went across the world in seconds. It was terrifying.

When it happened, it was also the end of the month, and the first of the month is when all my bills are due, including the mortgage. My husband is the main signer on everything, and since he was deployed, I couldn't stop anything. Basically, I was handcuffed because the banks couldn't stop anything, but they let me put my regular bills through, since those always cleared.

The bank told us that what we could do is cancel both cards, and reissue cards. Well, we couldn't do that when my husband was overseas because then he would have nothing.

It took months for them to track it, to stop it, to get money back to my account. Honestly, if it wasn't for the bank stopping it and telling me, it would've been far worse without the alerts.

That's why I'm a big believer in fraud alerts, because they knew exactly where I was at that moment, when it all started happening, so I didn't have to prove that it wasn't me.

At that time, my business was still new, so my debit card was connected to my business account and my checking account. When cybercriminals took that one number, they had access to everything, as soon as it over drafted it started pulling everything from the other accounts. Thank God I had another account that I could use.

I couldn't tell my husband what was going on because he was in a war zone, I couldn't just call and say, "Oh, dear, don't use your credit card".

Six months later when my husband was coming back from overseas, his card was immediately stolen. He used it once, and the process happened again, but the bank knew, and were already watching our account, they stopped his even faster.

Now we never use a debit card when traveling or in a store, we only use credit cards, because the bank can stop them right away. But we didn't know that, because we're cash people. We put money down with the mindset we're only going to use this specific amount, so that's why we used it the way we did, thinking we were safe.

I'm far more cautious with all my cards. I will not hand them over to anyone who says they want to do an impression of it, if that's the case, I will say, hold on, I'm going to an ATM, get cash, and then I'll come back. I don't care how big the store is, because this was a big reputable store that I was at, and they stole my card.

Even at a hotel, I do not let them take an impression of my card. We live in a digital world, for example we depend on our cellphones for personal and business reasons, and all cybercriminals need to do is access our phones and they have all of our information.

I also don't give my ID, driver's license, and my card at the same time. When someone calls and says they forgot to get the security code at the back of the card, I say no, "I'm not giving this information to you" and I won't email it to them either. I'm very cautious now.

When I went back to the store, the employee was nowhere to be found. I didn't want to point my finger at her and say 'you stole my card' until I knew it was really her. It could've been their system that she typed it into, for all I knew. I just went back, told the manager, this was the last place I was at, where the employee took an impression of my card, and my card was stolen. We never saw her again, and I never went back to that store again after that.

Summary

Credit and debit card fraud is a form of identity theft as Cybermonsters are using your card information for their gain. In addition to fraudulent purchases online or in stores, they could convert your cards into quick cash, buying gift cards, doing ATM withdrawals or selling them in bulk as part of a bigger cybercrime scheme.

Identity theft can happen to anyone. Veterans and military personnel are a target because their medical and government benefits are attractive to Cybermonsters. When active duty personnel are serving overseas it is more challenging to discover and resolve identity theft issues right away as in Michelle's husband's case.

Michelle has adopted excellent practices that allow her and her family to protect their most important information.

As card fraud rates continue to rise faster than ever, consider these three recommendations:

1. Place an Active Duty Alert on your credit report if you are on active military duty, because it adds an extra step to verify your identity before granting new credit under your name. This is a free service and it doesn't impact your credit score.
2. Activate alerts for your credit cards and bank accounts, so you receive a text or an email every time they are used. This allows you to identify if someone is doing a fraudulent transaction and take action immediately.
3. Use a second method to validate your identity on your most sensitive accounts. For example, using an authenticator app that gives you a new code every 30 seconds or receiving a code via email or text message.

If you or someone you know has become a victim of identity theft, report it to *IdentityTheft.gov*

A very inexpensive lesson!

Mari Smith

I'm a public speaker, renowned for speaking on Facebook marketing around the US and internationally. Companies interested in booking me to speak typically go to my website and fill out a form that asks them about their event.

My team and I received a form, thoroughly filled out, inviting me to speak at an event in Stockholm, Sweden. It was for The Persson Foundation; Mr. Stefan Persson is the chairman of H&M. The organization was planning a major red-carpet fundraising gala, and they wanted me to do the keynote.

I did some brief research, and it certainly seemed like an incredible and legitimate invitation. I saw and sensed zero red flags at the time. These types of invitations are fairly common for me.

The invitation was sent to me on March 4th and contained lots of details, including the types of dignitaries that would be there, first-class expenses all fully covered—the royal treatment, really. I did briefly think, "Gosh, why are they inviting me on the 4th to speak at an event on the 28th of the same month? It's a tight turnaround." Occasionally this does happen, where a major speaker backs out, for instance, and the host is looking to book a new speaker in short order. Or, the event suddenly got a big sponsor and has funds to book a keynote speaker.

At first, I consented to make the trip and we began negotiating fees and making plans. But within a week or so, because of the global crisis and the travel ban in place now, I explained to the contacts I would not be able to make the trip. They told me not to worry as they were pivoting to a virtual event, and they would like me to record a short video keynote. We continued discussions to do a paid video keynote, again negotiating fees. There were several parties involved in the email communications, including the Foundation's commercial director and legal advisor.

Then, by March 25th the team pivoted again to really raise the stakes; they were going to do a massive global fundraiser to help with the crisis. Mr. Stefan Persson is among the top 50 wealthiest people on the planet, with a net worth of over $20 billion. This team informed me that Mr. Persson had decided to put this major fundraiser together now. They wanted to raise $500 million, specifically for the direct benefit of people severely impacted by the global crisis in Africa, Asia, and Europe.

They were inviting celebrities, athletes and top entertainment and media icons to create short, uplifting videos to provide messages of hope. This all sounded wonderful and generous to me. I was so motivated to help. They offered me a full one-month media contract for use of the video. The team told me that the way this works is Mr. Persson gives me money to contribute back to the fundraiser. They were going to pay me my speaking fee for the video, and then provide an additional amount over and above my fee to donate to the mega fundraiser.

I just thought maybe this is one way that multi-billionaires operate; they move money around from one fund or cause to another. I actually thought they were being innovative; perhaps a creative way for optimizing taxable donation benefits. We proceeded with the contract and I signed it. We agreed on a $100,000 fee for original video creation and production, with a 5% agency fee. Plus, I negotiated an additional $100,000 budget for my team and I to place Facebook and Instagram ads for the Foundation. The paid promotion would help further raise awareness for the campaign and raise even more funds. I was really motivated to help them make a difference now. They agreed to these amounts, and proposed the amount for my charitable donation: a cool $250,000 to give back to the Foundation.

Grand total, $455,000. They asked me to submit my invoice for my video fees and the social media ads, but not to include the

$250,000 charity amount on the invoice as that was the donation back. Of course, my pertinent details are included on my invoice: bank account number, routing number, and business address. This is commonplace on all my invoices anyway. The team said they would be wiring the money to my account. I made sure to call my bank and alert them that this large sum was coming and explained the source. I also spoke with my attorney and my CPA, seeking proper advice on tax implications and anything else I needed to know. All was well and going smoothly, so far.

At this time, even though I still didn't sense any major red flags and had no clue something was really amiss, I didn't start on the video production, of course. I knew to wait for payment for certain. It's now April 7th and the team said the video was to be submitted by April 27th. Suddenly, they changed the payment method. Instead of wiring the funds, they told me their accountant in California would be mailing a check through FedEx overnight to my business address. They provided the FedEx tracking number and I could see when it was indeed delivered the next day.

To me, I just figured somehow a check must have been easier for them. However, my partner, Christopher, did think it was weird that they said they were going to wire the money and all of a sudden it was a check. But I just figured they're in Sweden, I'm in California and if they have an accountant in my state, maybe that was easier.

So, I drove down to my post office. At this stage, I had already been in lockdown for a month; I hadn't gone anywhere, not even to the store, as I'd stocked up in advance. I go to my post office, get the check, go to my drive-up banking, and deposit it. The teller did ask where I got the money; she wondered if I had just sold my house. I explained briefly what the payment was for and told her I'd been speaking with her colleague Bryan Rogers*, he knew all about it and all was fine. She confirmed the check was deposited now but they would be putting a hold on all but $5,000 of the funds for seven business days. I was fine with that. Again, not planning to take any action whatsoever until the funds had fully cleared. Not because I was suspicious of this team all being bad actors. But, because it's just good business sense to ensure funds clear for certain.

I deposited the check on Wednesday afternoon, and by late the next morning, Bryan at the bank called to say the whole thing was a fraud and it was a fake check. He told me their fraud department caught it. I'm thinking, *'Are you kidding me?!'* My brain simply could not comprehend what was happening at first. *'How could this be a fraud? How could I have been so foolish?'* I thought. There must be a mistake. Bryan told me the check wasn't even drawn on a real account, something about a wash. My brain was numb.

While I'm speaking with Bryan from the bank, I see a call waiting: it's a Stockholm number. I asked Bryan to hold on for a moment as here was The Persson Foundation calling me right now.

It was Chris, The Persson Foundation's legal advisor. *'Hello Mari? I just heard there's an issue with your bank. Are you able to use a different bank account?'* I wasn't sure what to say or think, and was confused, as I'm still not comprehending this could really be a big fraud. I went back to Bryan waiting on the other line. He confirmed it was absolutely a fraud. I was devastated. I couldn't believe that I had fallen for this sick and twisted scam, and that there are just awful people out there.

I've no idea how these scammers thought the check would clear; it was a totally fake check. They must rely on foolish people sending back the 'charitable donation' before the check clears properly. Or, hoping the banks don't detect the fake check. I certainly had zero intent of transferring any money out; I know enough to ensure funds clear first!

The scammers now have my bank information, since it was on my invoice. But now my account is frozen. I've been with the same bank for 20 years, but have to shut this account down, open up a new one and move all my vendors and bills. My bank said it's a precaution, mainly. The scammers could try and make fake checks now with my details and try to cash them. So, even though it was a big nuisance I took all the precautions per my bank's advice.

Now that this was all out in the open and I realized I'd been taken for a massive ride, I did more in-depth research that my staff and I ought to have done from day one. We discovered that the real name of Mr. Stefan Persson's foundation is actually H&M Foundation, it's not even called The Persson Foundation, though these scammers had a somewhat convincing website in that name.

And, there is a Facebook page in the name of the Persson family foundation in Swedish. I discovered a post pinned to the top from 2017 stating categorically that the Persson family foundation does not do 'Advance Fee Schemes.' The post has hundreds of comments from all manner of influencers, agencies and public figures who had also been contacted with similar offers over the years. Comment after comment states this is a scam. This broke my heart to realize that these people have been trying to take advantage of innocent people for years and seemingly have not been caught yet.

At the end of the day, my partner told me, '*Mari, you've had a very inexpensive lesson. The universe taught you a lesson, and it didn't cost you anything.*' True. I didn't even lose a dime. I just temporarily lost my pride. Hindsight is 20/20. And, yes, I can now see many tiny little red flags, some louder than others, but my brain just didn't want to believe it. I was caught up in the flurry of such an exciting project, to be in a position to make such a big contribution for a good cause. This experience has definitely put me on my guard now. And, I hope others can learn from me sharing it.

Not his real name

Summary

Scammers and Cybermonsters are always looking for ways to trick you into disclosing sensitive personal information or financial data.

One of the techniques is establishing a conversation or an exchange of information because it is likely to create a more believable narrative.

A fake check looks like a regular check - it could be printed with legitimate financial information or could even be a real check that belongs to other identity theft victims, they are a form of a scam designed to wire money back as banks must make funds from deposited checks available within days, and sometimes uncovering a fake check could take several weeks.

Mari had a great relationship with her bank, and as she involved different people to ensure a safe transaction, she realized on time that it wasn't real. Is it too good or bad to be true? Then, it's probably not true at all!

Consider these three recommendations:

1. Establish a relationship with your bank, ask how their processes work, and always talk to someone you trust before acting on a new transaction that came through an online contact. Scams could include check funds converted into gift cards, money orders, or wire money. Don't rely on money from a check unless you know and can validate the source.
2. Research any charity donation request received online. The safest is to go to the non-profit organization's website and donate directly. Using your credit card is the safest way to donate. Always double check the name of the charity or non-profit organization to ensure it is spelled correctly.
3. Be aware of someone rushing you to take action, either in an email or phone call, because scammers use pressure as a tactic to overwhelm you and steal your money or information.

Report scams to the Federal Trade Commission *ftc.gov/complaint*. For international scams report it to *eConsumer.gov*, they are an organization in partnership with more than 35 consumer protection agencies around the world. This is the best way we can help authorities spot scam trends and combat fraud.

We've got full control of your computer!

Paul Wakefield

Founder of Freedom Lifestyle Academy

I'm from the U.K, living just outside of London, and I've had an online business now since 2008, I work as a business coach. The online world has completely changed my life, it's allowed me to become an author, a speaker, I've trained and coached thousands of people around the world.

For me, working online is an everyday thing. It's what I've always done.

One evening, in maybe late 2015, I was working at home, and I had just moved back to my hometown. I was using the spare room in my mum and dad's house as an office. That particular evening my parents went out, so I worked a little bit later than I normally do, closed the computer, went downstairs, started doing some dinner, put a bit of TV on, and then I had a message from Facebook messenger pop up.

It was from a friend connection. The message said, 'Hi Paul, I hope you're well - I've been following you for several years now, love what you do. I'm in High Wickham tomorrow, I need help with my business. Is there any chance we could meet?'

Normally, I wouldn't reply. I may post a bit on social media in the evenings, but I definitely don't do work.

I replied and asked where she was going to be. She said it'd be great to meet up for a coffee in Town Center. She told me she needed help with her website and growing the business.

I'm very strict in regard to meetings. My clients must take a questionnaire to qualify them before I meet anybody. I asked her if she could just go on and answer these few questions, to find out a bit more about her and then we'll meet up.

She said, "Well, I really need your help now, can you jump on a videoconference now?" It's past 7 in the evening, my day's kind of finished, so I asked her to answer these questions. She was really adamant that she wanted to meet me and wanted my help. She said, "no, let's just jump on the video call now." So, I thought, "forget it, let's jump on the videoconference". So, I said "send me the link and we'll jump on it, and we'll have a quick call."

I went upstairs, turned the computer on, loaded the video call, and we jumped on it. This blonde lady sat there, in her office, and I kept it really short and sweet, and asked "what are you struggling with?" She said, "Well, just overall about my business." And I ask specifically, "what is she struggling with." Suddenly the screen went black.

I started saying, "Hello? Is anyone there? Can you hear me?" And then this lady came back, and she was completely naked from head to toe. And I said, "Woah, woah, woah, who's this, what's going on?"

She said, "I've been following you for ages, I don't want your help with business." I didn't want this, so I went to end the call and it wouldn't let me end it. I went to end it again. I told this lady, "I can't end the call, can you just end the call? I'm not interested."

Suddenly it went completely black, then I saw this figure of a foreign man, he was very dark, and I couldn't see his face. This voice says, "We've got your computer now, and we're in control."

I went to end the call again and it wouldn't end, and then the voice came back again and said, "We've got full control of your computer, you cannot end this call."

This lady comes back on, completely naked, she said, "I know you've got tattoos, show me your tattoos." She told me to take off my shirt and show her the tattoos on my chest, and I said, "No, I'm not taking my shirt off, I don't know you."

Then the voice came back that said, "We have full control. We have control of your social media, we have control of your computer, do as we say or there will be trouble." The gal said she knew I had tattoos on my waistline next to the stomach, and she said, "I want to see those tattoos." Now I'm panicking and by now I've been on this call for 45 minutes. I just showed them one of my tattoos so they could just about see it, near my thigh.

They sent me a screen grab, and because of the way I stood up and I pulled my T-shirt up a little bit, and I sort of put my hand down the side of my pants to show the tattoo, they said, "We now have a screen grab of you touching yourself." I hadn't done anything! They threatened me to upload this to social media and all over the Internet. I kept on saying, "No, that's not what's happened."

I said, "Look, I don't know who you are, I don't know what you want, but that's not what happened, I'm turning the computer off now," and suddenly when I was about to turn it off, my phone started to go mad with Facebook notifications.

That picture they had created was uploaded onto my Facebook, and they had tagged me in hundreds of inappropriate photos on Facebook, saying something along the lines of, 'Warning: be careful of this person, this is what he does.'

I quickly deleted them on my phone, and I thought, maybe if I delete the lady from Facebook, this will end, so then I deleted her as a Facebook friend and blocked her. This figure comes back up on the computer, and said, "You just deleted and blocked us on Facebook, undelete us and unblock us, or we will make your life hell," and I said, "No, I'm not doing anything, I've done what you wanted, you're not a friend." The man says, "Make us a friend again, unblock us, or else."

Suddenly, I could see on the screen all my friend's and family's information; my mom's email, my dad's name, sister's name, daughter's name, friends and they said, "We know where you are, we'll come and get you, and we'll hurt your family." I unblocked them, they literally did have me trapped, and I said, "What do you want? Stop this."

They said they wanted 30,000 or 50,000 pounds. And they said, "We know you've got money; we know you're a successful businessman, send over the money now, and we won't push this video or this image any further," and I said "No," so they started to post on Facebook again. By now I was probably on the call for 4 hours, really panicking trying to turn off the computer.

My mom and dad had been out of the house this whole time, and when it was getting close to midnight, they came back. I told them I had a last-minute call, and then a message came up that said, "if you say anything to them, we will hurt your family."

I told the guy, "Enough is enough now, this had been going on for 4 or 5 hours, you made your point, but I've got nothing to give you, you're certainly not getting 30,000 from me." They told me to make the transaction, pay now or we'll hurt your family. I said, "I haven't got that sort of money." They replied that they knew I had that money and that I was a successful businessperson.

I have a variety of different bank accounts and I've had different addresses over the years, so I mixed the information using different numbers and I said, "It's not working."

They told me to prove it, so I took screen grabs, and sent it to them. I said, "I'll try a smaller amount first and see if that works." I tried sending 1,000 pounds with the combination of all different things, knowing that it wouldn't work, and I told them it was still not working.

They were getting really angry and they started posting all over again, saying, "This is going everywhere, it's going viral, we will finish you, we will finish your business, we've tagged pictures of you to your daughter," and it went on until about 1 am, and I said, "I'm physically and mentally done, I'm trying to give you the money, it's not working, please just leave me alone or I will go to the police."

Then that was it, the call and everything turned off. I sat there for about 10-15 minutes waiting for things to come back up and it didn't. I went on social media, I cleared everything. After I cleared my YouTube, I went to bed at about 2am. I pretty much cried myself to sleep, I had never felt so scared in my life. I woke up in the morning, and I went straight to the police station.

When I went to bed the previous night, I searched what had happened to me, to see if it had happened previously, and I found a story online of a young lad who had something similar happen to him, and sadly, he took his life. It freaked me out, but I could completely understand why because it was so traumatic. I felt dirty, and it was a disgusting, horrible feeling.

I walked into the police station and explained the situation. They took all my computers away and I was unable to be online for two weeks. I still had my phone, luckily, so I was able to ask a friend of mine, to add a message to my Facebook group with members and clients to tell people I was offline.

The police followed up within the next seven days, came up to the house 2 or 3 times, and kept interviewing me. Eventually, I told my parents what had happened, they were scared and devastated. And the case went on for a few months.

Sadly, they never found them, but what they did trace it back to a gang operating in a very small island, which sadly is known for this.

I changed the way I operate my business online, qualifying my clients, asking them to complete questions ahead of time, paying a refundable deposit in advance and I sent the link to our meetings. Also, I'm very careful with who I connect on Facebook. It's actually helped my business.

The police told me if I wasn't so aware and Internet savvy, this could've been so much worse.

We have 3 daughters, we're very careful about where they go and what they're doing, but we don't live in fear. I think when you start being scared, it has a negative impact on your cyber world. You've just got to be sensible. Be aware of what you do and how you interact with technology. Things can happen, but don't be scared, take action to protect your data, your family and your business.

Summary

Infected links with malware allow Cybermonsters to install software to infect your computer and grant them access to your information.

In Paul's story, the motive was financial gain using an extortion scam, threatening and blackmailing for payment. This story teaches many lessons, one that stands out, and that Paul highlights really well, is choosing not to be scared and focusing more on the actions you can take to protect your cyber world.

Having mental strength as well as communicating what is happening to you to someone you trust and to law enforcement officials is key. There are many resources available that can help you navigate an identity theft or an extortion situation and potentially prevent others from going through the same situation because you are raising awareness.

When we share our cyber stories, we connect at a personal level, and it helps us realize how real and devastating identity theft and cybercrime can be to us personally and to our business. At the same time, it shares the message that we can recover from it.

We have the power to choose happiness, even if we are facing tough times. It doesn't necessarily mean you are smiling, it means taking action, because it is the only way we can protect our data, our family and our business from hackers, scammers and Cybermonsters and it is the way we can live *Happily Ever Cyber!*

Consider these three recommendations:

1. An infected link could be received in many different ways, as an email, text, social media, and even could be embedded in pictures. Pay special attention if someone is urging you to click on a link. Instead of clicking on a link, go to your Internet browser and type directly the address of the website you want to visit.

2. Create an account in your computer that doesn't have admin privileges meaning that software cannot be installed unless you type the admin user and password. Use a regular

user account for your daily activities such as email, surfing the Internet and working.

3. Before accepting someone in your social media profiles, research who they are and check their profiles, if you note you don't have common friends or they don't have much information on their profiles and are randomly inviting you to connect without knowing you, why would you take that risk?

Report related Internet crimes to the *FBI Crime Complaint Center (IC3.gov)*, contact your *local law enforcement*, and for international scams report it to *eConsumer.gov*, they are in a partnership with more than 35 consumer protection agencies around the world. This is the best way you can help authorities because your story can help track patterns of fraud and stop Cybermonsters.

If you are experiencing distress, call the prevention and crisis resources at the *National Suicide Prevention Hotline 1-800-273-8255* or at *suicidepreventionlife.org*. It is a 24x7 free service.

In the UK, contact the *Samaritans.org*. They also have a free 24x7 service for you to call or email.

Another Cyber Story!

You may be familiar with scams; they could happen during a conversation with a live person, or throughout a recorded message inviting you to press a key in your phone to continue and engage you in a dialog.

Scammers have figured out countless ways to trick us with the purpose to steal our money, by acting friendly and helpful, in other cases threatening or even manipulating our emotions.

Common scams may include receiving a phone call indicating your social security number has been compromised, and that you could be facing criminal charges.

Scammers may contact you asking to call back to resolve an IRS (Internal Revenue Services) dispute. You may have received a phone call indicating you have won a prize, or have been selected for an incredible offer, or that you have won the lottery, without you even buying a ticket!

Scammers may also pretend to help you or your business by offering lower interest credit card rates, fixing your credit, or getting your student or mortgage loan forgiven if you pay them a fee. They may promise to help you start your new business and guarantee big profits for an investment opportunity once you invest first in what they are offering. Or they could offer you a free trial for a product or services and then you are billed monthly until you remember to cancel the service.

In the following story, Jack focuses on what could have happened and how his awareness was the key to stop and prevent a scam to his family.

Opt out now!

Jack Canfield

America's #1 Success Coach

Cybersecurity. It's something not everyone talks about every day, but they need to be talking about it.

It almost touched my family. I walked in on my wife one afternoon and she was on the phone with someone from India.

I asked her, "What's going on?"

And she said, "I got this message that there was a virus in my computer, and I called the number." The guy on the phone was just about to say, 'will you let me take control of your computer?'

And I said, "No way! Opt out now". And she opted out.

Cybercrime can be so sophisticated. You think the government, or the IRS is contacting you. That someone wants to send you money from Nigeria. Some situations are obvious, but some of them are really sophisticated so you have to be really aware.

Summary

Scammers and Cybermonsters are always looking for ways to get your information. During tech support scams they want to access your computer and pretend to run a test. They may ask for payment to fix a problem that didn't exist in the first place. Scammers may try to use a pop-up window on your computer screen indicating they have "detected suspicious activity" and listing a phone number to call.

Another tactic used is a fake refund scam, offering you a refund for services you paid for or indicating the company is going out of business and they are giving out refunds. Scammers are trying to get more money out of you and steal your banking information. Jack did exactly what needs to be done in this kind of situation; simply hang up!

Consider these three recommendations:

1. Ignore pop-up windows, links, texts or emails that ask you to take immediate action to fix your computer. Legitimate companies are not going to call you and ask for your user and password information. Hang up if you get these calls.
2. Imagine you have several holes in the walls of your home and anyone could sneak through those holes and show up in your living room. Would you fix these holes? In the same way, your phone and computers are full of holes when programs or the apps you use are not updated regularly, and they could expose you to scammers and Cybermonsters. Keep your technology safe by updating computers and phones.
3. Using mindfulness is one of your best defenses against hackers, scammers and Cybermonsters. When we are present using technology, we don't simply react to click, open or give information about our cyber world.

Report scams to the *Federal Trade Commission (FTC.gov/complaint)* and report any suspected Internet-facilitated criminal activity to the *FBI Crime Complaint Center (IC3.gov)* because your story could make the difference to prevent someone from becoming a victim and contribute to stopping scammers and Cybermonsters.

Now it is your turn!

From the stories you read, which one resonated most with you? Why?

From the recommendations listed in each of the stories, select three that you commit to applying right away. Remember that taking action is how you can protect what matters most to you!

Notes

What are the big takeaways for you in this chapter?

| |
| |
| |
| |
| |
| |
| |
| |

It's Never Too Late to Live
Happily Ever Cyber!

A s our digital world is constantly changing and evolving, Cyber-monsters continue to find creative ways to keep growing their lucrative business to steal our information, our identities, and so much more. That is the reality of the cyberworld we live in.

This is why it is so important that we change how we perceive and approach cybersecurity, cybercrime, and identity theft.

There are many actions you and I can take together to reduce the chances of you becoming a victim of cybercrime or identity theft.

I want you to get excited and inspired about cybersecurity now that you know there is more that you can do beyond just hard technical steps. Together we can start our journey to simplify cybersecurity to become second nature to you.

- Now that you know the basics about the Cybermonsters and you have assessed yourself, are you confident and ready to start protecting yourself, your business, and family?
- Have I encouraged you to incorporate these changes into your life?

- Are you motivated to create your own stories to help reduce the chance for you or your family to become a victim of cybercrime or identity theft?
- Are you open to discovering a canvas of opportunities to navigate the cyber ocean?
- Are you ready to protect what really matters most to you from hackers, scammers and Cybermonsters?

What we have covered so far in this book is the beginning of our journey together as we take care of the basics to navigate the cyberworld, understanding the Why, What, and How - we are no longer an easy target for cybercrime or identity theft.

How did I start my scuba diving journey? By taking care of the basics so I could enjoy the ocean and its wonderful possibilities.

Once upon a time I was terrified of dying in the water and that fear was transformed into my love for scuba diving and all the beauty the ocean offers.

In the same way, I invite you to take the necessary steps and cultivate the skills to navigate the cyber ocean. Then you can really enjoy all the wonderful things we can do online because this world is full of amazing things.

As we continue our journey to enjoy all the wonderful things we can do online, learning the fundamentals provides us with the confidence to keep ourselves, our business, and our families safe, protecting what matters most to us.

What excites me the most is to help you on your cybersecurity journey because my stories are about conquering our fears, dreaming big, and choosing happiness.

"Everything you look at can become a fairy tale and you can get a story from everything you touch."
  – Hans Christian Andersen - Once Upon A Time!

After my weekend adventure to become a certified scuba diver, I returned home thinking that was the last time I would be in the ocean and that scuba diving was not for me. Jorge was wrong. I did not see the most beautiful thing in the world.

Yes, I completed the Open Water Diver PADI certification, but my fear of the water was still there as well as my mom's words, "If you are ever near the water, you are going to die." Of course, I did not die but I almost let someone else die.

On Monday morning, I went to let my friend Jen know that I was not going on the scuba diving trip I had already paid and signed up for before my certification in the open water. This trip included Jorge, Al, Jen, and a few other experienced scuba divers in our group.

"Jen, I am not going on this trip. Scuba diving is not for me."

Jen said, "Well, Sandra, I understand but if you back out the whole trip will be canceled as there is a mandatory requirement to have a certain number of people on the sailing yacht. This is a commitment we have already made so you cannot cancel now."

"Ok, Jen, I will go, but I won't do any scuba diving for sure."

On Friday after our workday, we drove for about four hours to the sailing port. Our adventure would be in Las Aves Archipelago, which is part of the Federal Dependencies of Venezuela in the Caribbean Sea. At the port, I learned that we needed to ride in a dinghy boat to get to the sailing yacht that was a few miles away.

My heartbeat started going faster as I sat in the dinghy boat. At nighttime, the ocean is pitch black. I held on to my life jacket so tightly as if my life depended on it. Well, it certainly did.

My breathing stopped when someone mentioned that we would be sailing all night since Las Aves was 12 hours away. Why do I never ask for the details before saying "yes"?

The sunrise was gorgeous. The red and yellow tones were reflecting on the water, the blue sky was amazing. The whole view looks like a postcard that I saw when I was a kid. I felt a fresh breeze on my face and then I remembered, "Uh-oh, we are on the open sea. Where is my life jacket?"

We were having breakfast sitting around a dinette table finished in maple with mahogany accents. The entire room was quite beautifully decorated in crafted wood. There was a bookcase full of books on the main wall of the room. In the upper corner, there was an artificial sunflower arrangement that matches the decor perfectly. On the opposite side, there was a small collection of sand clocks. Everyone was so excited about the scuba diving adventure that was about to start.

The group gears-on with their scuba equipment and some of them were even carrying cameras and external flash dive lights, also known as strobes. As I observed everyone, they take a giant stride putting the regulator in their mouths while holding the regulator and mask with their palm. They lifted one leg out in front and jumped into the water. In a few seconds, they were all floating in the water.

The sailing boat or ketch was from Finland and its name was "Kulkuri." The ketch is a two-masted sailboat. It was about 90 ft. long. I am not sure what the freeboard or distance was from the waterline to the upper deck where I was standing but the water was not near. I said to myself, "There is no way I would ever jump from here."

I stayed on the deck. As I was contemplating the day, Angie, the captain's daughter, asked me, "Sandra, why aren't you going with your friends? Aren't you a scuba diver?"

I told her about my last weekend experience while getting my certification and how Al almost died because I was holding his hand and I didn't know how to swim. I said, "Angie, scuba diving is not for me; besides, nobody will ever hold my hand again."

Angie smiled, and with the sweetest voice, she said, "I am a certified scuba diver instructor and I will hold your hand, if you want to try again. We can practice the basics again and teach you how to be neutrally buoyant. If you still think that scuba diving is not for you, then at least you have tried in one of the prettiest places in the world. Do you want to try?"

Jorge was right. This was the most beautiful and fascinating thing in the world! I was slightly moving my body underwater; my legs were moving up and down in opposite directions but very softly and slowly. This must be what we would feel if we had wings and could fly. There was no gravity in the water, I felt weightless.

There was no noise. It was very peaceful and relaxing. I only heard my own breathing and the air bubbles coming from my regulator, they were so pretty.

I saw the most intense blue water with all the vibrant colors around me and the incredible coral reefs, the plants, the sea creatures, and all the fish swimming around me.

Was I dreaming?

No, I was not. I was still holding Angie's hand. I had just fallen in love with scuba diving.

I came back from this trip and signed up for swimming lessons right away and my scuba diving adventures had just started.

Give me your hand - our new journey together is about to start to live *Happily Ever Cyber!*

―⊶✻⊷―

"Actually, the best gift you could have given her was a lifetime of adventures."

Lewis Carroll – Alice in Wonderland

―⊶✻⊷―

A Lifetime of Adventures

After working for the same global company for several years, our family was relocated from Venezuela to the United States to a city in the Midwest. Yes, I know, it is cold there! Starting a new chapter with my husband Ricardo was full of excitement for the unknown that was waiting for us in a land far, far away. And for me, it included a new position as an Information Technology Consultant.

Getting used to the culture, and to working, driving, and socializing was much easier than getting used to the weather.

The job was going great. I got promoted several times and was given more management responsibilities.

A few years had passed, and it was time to take on my next chapter, so I enrolled in an MBA program near Chicago. Classes were full days every Saturday, which allowed me to keep working during the week.

Only a few months into the program, my boss John asked me, "Hey Sandra, do you want to take on a new opportunity and lead a portion of a major project initiative company-wide? This will be great visibility for your career. Of course, you still need to do your full-time job as this project will be part-time only."

I responded, "Yes, I can do it."

My plate got full quickly. I reprioritized my life, stopped exercising, cooking, and limited my social time. I also reduced my sleep time to two or three hours a day. I was always in a hurry.

Fast-forward two years: I graduated with honors, and the major project also ended with high success.

However, the next day after the graduation ceremony, I was unable to get out of bed. I crashed and mostly slept for an entire week. Then I went back to work and kept pushing forward, but something was different, something felt odd inside of me.

During the next few months, my health continued to decline. Not only was I very tired and felt pain, I was also dizzy, and unable to sleep.

Sometimes at night, I stared at the ceiling the whole night, feeling like my brain was swollen and unable to shut down and rest.

During the wintertime, driving back from the office, I felt very dizzy again. I pulled over and took my shoes off, so I could feel the gas and brake pedals better. I also opened all the windows in my car because the cold wind in my face forced me to remain focused. I stopped at the nearest walk-in clinic and my blood pressure was extremely low.

Doctors gave me prescriptions to stay awake, go to sleep, for pain, etc. There was no explanation as my basic lab reports were within normal ranges.

One time, I woke up in the middle of the night and I was in pain and felt very weak and dizzy. I woke Ricardo up, and the next moment, I passed out. I woke up again, and then I was in the Emergency Room and two nurses were trying to draw blood to run tests... The needles hurt.

As passing out happened a few more times in the ER, I was sent to ICU for observation and more tests.

A few days later, I left the hospital with several prescriptions to take including a heart medication. And without any logical explanation or knowing what was really going on, I went home.

When I finally started a quest to find answers, I visited several doctors who had very different opinions and diagnoses. I only got more new prescriptions. I was not getting any better, but I continued to work trying to pretend that nothing was happening.

Finally, the last doctor I visited decided to test beyond the obvious. He did complete blood work and found several deficiencies including vitamin B, D, and Iodine and other minerals that compromised different systems in my body. My adrenal system was not working, and my hormone production was extremely low which explained some of the symptoms.

Doctor SG said, "Sandra, cortisol helps to fuel your fight-or-flight system. It is like your natural alarm system. However, when cortisol levels are too high for longer periods of time and you are under constant stress, this alarm doesn't always turn off causing several issues in the body and affecting your immune system's response."

Doctor SG's approach was more holistic. He planted a seed in my brain to explore natural alternatives to my condition.

As I understood the What and the Why of what was happening to my body, I started to realize that the last two years of constant stress were major factors that contributed to my health issues. Once again, I remembered my promise to choose happiness no matter what and declared, "I am going to get my health back." I only needed to figure out How.

Entering the journey to recover my health removing toxins and eating only certain foods, I changed my lifestyle completely.

My husband Ricardo was there for me every moment in this journey. He cheered me up when I needed it most. Having him holding my hand gave me the strength to keep going to get my health back.

On one occasion, I didn't want to get up out of bed, or eat or do anything and Ricardo dragged me out of the house. We went to a dog park and since I am afraid of dogs, being there definitely woke-up my self-protection instincts. I was able to get out of my lethargic state.

It took me some time until my health was fully restored, all medications were gone and a "new" me was reborn. During this process, I moved from Information Technology and joined the cyber-security Team.

There were several reasons why I lost my health. The most important one was prioritizing everything else except me and making the choices that contributed to my body crisis including not taking care of the basics: my nutrition, hydration, exercise, sleep, and more. I took for granted our most precious gift and experienced the consequences of my decisions.

When I think about how my health crisis is similar to cybersecurity, and why it matters, if we do not take care of the basics (protecting our passwords, limiting the use of our location services, understanding the meaning of "free", making the choice of how much personal information we post online in social media, and much more to be covered in the rest of the *Happily Ever Cyber!* books in the series,) we put ourselves at risk. We take for granted the gift to navigate the cyberworld safely.

As we have covered in these pages, the consequences to our business, our families, or to ourselves, of being a victim of cybercrime or identity theft can take a long time to recover from, and in some cases, it might not even be possible.

When I lost my identity because a Cybermonster in China was using my information smuggling women into the United States and when I lost my health, both situations could be perceived as I was out of control and the odds were playing against me.

However, I have learned that we always have a choice because we are the architects of our own lives. I have also learned that having someone who we can rely on is very important. Throughout every experience of my life, there was always someone holding my hand and helping me conquer my fears.

What choices are you going to make?

How will you protect yourself, your business, and your family from cybercrime or identity theft?

Are you ready to prioritize and protect what is most important to you?

Will you take my hand?

Remembering once again my promise to choose happiness and to take action for the changes I wanted to see in my life and in this cyberworld, I left my corporate job, and founded my own company, Way2Protect, with the dream of using my personal stories to inspire and encourage you.

My goal is to make cybersecurity simple and give you the basics so you can protect yourself against hackers, scammers and Cyber-monsters and start our quest together to live *Happily Ever Cyber!*

About the *Happily Ever Cyber!*™ Foundation Dream

When I was less than one month old, my mom left me with my grandparents, who had eleven more kids and were living in extreme poverty. She moved far away to find a job and support me financially. I was told my father didn't want to know about me during that time.

One day, when I was four or five years old, a woman came by my grandparents' house and said my mother sent her to get me. We traveled several days in an old bus. The seats were made of plastic, and they were so worn out the fabric was coming off. The bus windows couldn't be opened and the temperature inside was hot. "I felt suffocating most of the time."

I became ill as we came close to our destination. We were sleeping on the street of an alley. A man came and asked for my name, saying he was going to take me to my mom. The woman who brought me sent her daughter, Nancy, in my place, because she wanted her to cross the border safely.

Finally, after the mix up, I reached my destination, and started a new life with my mom, and a stepfather in the picture. The following 15 years included abuse, loneliness, and deprivation. During those years I also had times of love, courage, empowerment, joy, teamwork, gratitude, and I was able to take action towards my dreams.

"He now felt glad at having suffered sorrow and trouble, because it enabled him to enjoy so much better all the pleasure and happiness around him."

— Hans Christian Andersen — The Ugly Duckling

Did you know the cybersecurity industry has a shortage of talent? [11]

Did you know the headcount gap is equivalent to fill fifty NFL stadiums? [11]

Did you know the cybersecurity unemployment rate in the US has been zero percent since 2011?[11]

The industry predicts millions of jobs will remain unfilled in the years to come and, as we have covered, Cybermonsters are not likely to stop and cybercrime will remain a top issue as they are increasing, not only in volume but also in complexity.

In our cyber world, technical skills are essential, and they can be developed through traditional education methods as well as self-taught, curiosity and a technical ability. Now more than ever, we have access to unlimited information.

We can simply do a Google search and see millions of pages indexed with the topic we are searching for. With the use of social media tools, we now have access to connect and follow top talent, individuals, and companies. The bigger our cyber world, the bigger the opportunity in front of us.

Did you know there are over 153 million orphans in the world? An estimated 5,700 children become orphans every day. [12]

Did you also know in the US, there are almost half a million kids in the foster care system? [12]

I was not an orphan nor did I live in the foster care system, but I know what it is like to feel lonely and abandoned.

An orphanage is a place where many children are cared for by skilled adults. In the US orphanages have been replaced by the Foster Care System. The concept consists of one family taking in one or more children into their home for short- or long-term care.

According to UNICEF, ninety-five per cent of all orphans are over the age of five[12]. The median age of children in the foster care system is six and a half years old. Approximately fourteen million children turning eighteen years old are taken out of the orphanage system. Roughly thirty thousand young adults age out of the foster care system every year. [12]

If children remain in the foster care system or in the orphanages until they age out of the system, their possibilities of having a life with the necessary tools, skills, knowledge, resources and purpose can be very limited.

These new adults could be forced into human trafficking, suffer higher rates of substance abuse, mental illness, teen pregnancy, homelessness, and arrests because they are unprepared and unable to support themselves.

I believe there are multiple ways to solve our talent shortage in Cybersecurity and in other areas and at the same time solve the much bigger problem we have in the world with orphans and foster kids [12].

I was blessed that mentors showed up early in and throughout my life in different ways and forms, as my school teachers, sport coaches, classmates, teammates, coworkers, bosses, and even strangers provided guidance or a word of wisdom during times when I needed them the most.

My teacher Roxane used to say this phrase over and over "to whom much is given, much will be required". When I think of all the blessings and gifts I have received in my life, my gratitude list is pretty extensive, so this phrase remains as a pillar and my mantra to this day.

My dream is to create the *Happily Ever Cyber!* Foundation. I want to provide orphans and foster care kids a way to find themselves, their stories, and their inspiration by leveraging the use of technology. I do not know the *How* yet, but I am committed to figuring it out!

Acknowledgments

⸺⟡⸺

To Dave Tyson for believing in me, and supporting me to enter the amazing world of cybersecurity.

Thank you to Pamela Fusco for always encouraging me to navigate the Cyber world. Love you!

To Jeff Spivey for your mentorship in cybersecurity and for always caring about Venezuela.

To every Homeland Security, CBP and TSA agent I have ever met in my journey.

To Randy Bowman, Dennis Lloyd, Alejandro Briceno, Marta Estaba and John Mandli, you all believed in me and made my life of possibilities, be possible. Thank you!

To David Flores for being my greatest friend and for helping me go through my college degree.

To Elayna Fernandez, Story Strategist, and overall Marketing, PR and Branding expert that made possible to create the *Happily Ever Cyber!* series. To Elisha Fernandez, Line Editor and Illustrator of the book. To Barb Hollace for her copy-editing support and her blessings.

To Jack Canfield, Steve Harrison, and Patty Aubery for sharing your wisdom and knowledge.

To Sandra and Kim Yancey for creating an amazing platform. To the eWomen Network Milwaukee and the Platinum community. To Jamie Shibley and my SOAR sisters.

To Bo Eason, Dawn Eason, Colleen Hauk, and the rest of the Eason's team. To my Masterminds Warriors and to the Best!

To Jeffrey Bornman, beyond your coaching and guidance, I am so grateful for you.

To Jean-Loui Rodrigue for your coaching and for helping me find my eagle's wisdom.

To Craig Duswalt for all your branding coaching and the Mastermind and Elite group's support.

To Jeffrey Peterson and the Leads Inc. team for our exciting journey ahead.

To Lance Spitzner for introducing to the fascinating world of Cyber Training & Awareness

To my Accounting and Finance teams that are helping me build my dream business.

To Mari Smith, Michelle Mras, Paul Wakefield, Tim, and Vicky L. for sharing their cyber stories to inspire you to protect what matters to you.

To Bozena Kalita, James Lim, Mark Ward, Steve Langer, Paula Powell, and John and Amy Roufus for reading my draft book and giving me your input, recommendations and testimonial.

To all my IT, cybersecurity and data privacy friends, co-workers, and everyone that I have learned from throughout my journey.

Special thank you to Lindsay Edgar, Ataikor Ngerebara, Alexa Smith, Mike Borromeo, Emma Peace, Gareth Venables, Mike Weisman, Daniela Seitz, Andy Nissenberg and Tim Lynam for the journey shared at Stericycle.

Thank you to my teachers, doctors, friends, co-workers, classmates, and others who help me throughout my journey. I have learned from each of you and we have shared great moments of joy and pain.

To my family and extended family. To my Mom, Muriel, Edward and Camilo and to Elmer. To my cousin Adriana, my aunties Gloria, Alba, Nora, Dora, Noelba. To Lio and Adriana; Enrique and Yone. To Liito, Barbarita, Kike, Bichito, Michin and Elydia. To Coro and the Perez family; Eleo and Mark; Bea, Adri and Randolf; Zaida and Andres; Ada and Ruben; Pedro and Mayuco; Nade and Federico; Isa and Luis; Lianna and Oscar; Joe and Gisela; Aldo, Chucho; Gustavo and Yleny; Rafael and Maritza; Diana, Joe and the Nowak family; Ryan and Christy; Catalina, Sarah, Paulette, Ana Lucia, Christine, Nancy; Everlyn, Andrea, Alexandra and Pajarito; Zuleima, Mary and Monch; Annette and Mike; Jose Felix; Patricia and Alejandro; Bill and Lisa; Franz, Josefina, Maricruz, Yesenia, Daniela, Nuria, Aidee, Raiza, Ricardo, Dinora, Leonor, and Luis.

To my husband Ricardo, thank you for helping me capture the essence of my stories, for reading all my drafts and listening to them thousands of times. I love you.

Thank you "mi Dios" for everything you have given me, for all the blessings of my life. You are my inspiration and the reason to create this book.

About Sandra Estok

andra is a speaker, best seller author and corporate trainer. Through her publications, Sandra is committed to share her journey, her experience, and expertise using simple concepts and inspirational stories to help others protect what most matters to them against hackers, scammers and Cybermonsters.

She brings over twenty years of multicultural and cross-functional experience in the US, Latin America and Europe in the areas of cybersecurity, IT, and Data Privacy. Throughout her career, Sandra has held numerous positions in Fortune 500 companies, private and public organizations.

Sandra has developed and deployed capability, training and awareness programs, focusing on the *Why*, the *What* and the *How* of cyber threats, its dangers, and solutions, while making cybersecurity simple. She holds an MBA and industry certifications in IT, cybersecurity and Data Privacy.

Sandra believes that together we can change the way we perceive this cyber world and live *Happily Ever Cyber!*

Sandra is also passionate about yoga, meditation, cycling, and working out. She enjoys the outdoors every opportunity she has, she has re-learned how to cook using natural ingredients and she has recreated all her favorite recipes into healthier alternatives. Sandra lives with her husband, Ricardo in the Midwest.

Visit SandraEstok.com

About Way2Protect and *Happily Ever Cyber!*

The day after Sandra officially left the corporate world, she and her husband Ricardo went to Melbourne Beach, Florida to relax for a few days. During the second night, Sandra went to their beachfront hotel's patio to enjoy the beautiful night and meditate on her new life as an entrepreneur.

As the fresh breeze touched her face and she enjoyed the soothing sound of the ocean that once terrified her, she contemplated the sky full of stars. Suddenly, Sandra wondered which of the constellations was the Milky Way. She had never learned astronomy, she reflected, pondering on her biggest strengths, her true nature, and passions... what mattered most to her.

The word "protect" popped into Sandra's head and then she said, "Way to Protect." And in the next moment, Way2Protect LLC was born.

Sandra started focusing on developing her business and brand and while at an event surrounded by enthusiastic, and successful entrepreneurs; the memories of her life and the energy in the room, inspired her to write the *Happily Ever Cyber!* book series.

Way2Protect was founded to fulfill a simple yet powerful vision purpose:

"To change the way this cyberworld is perceived, simplifying cybersecurity, by leveraging our personal stories, relating and connecting us to protect what matters most against hackers, scammers and Cybermonsters, and together live *Happily Ever Cyber!*"

Way2Protect values and commitments are to:

1. **Choose Happiness no matter what;** even if we are facing tough times.
2. **Take action.** Dreams and declarations are important, yet it is our actions that make them possible.
3. **Inspire and encourage** our customers, our partners, our employees and our communities to change the way we perceive this cyber world.
4. **Foster integrity.** Honesty, open communication, and loyalty are the pillars for everything we do.
5. **Create win-win partnerships.** Our partners, vendors and sponsors align with our commitment to protect individuals, communities and the environment.
6. **Thrive together.** Being a reliable, responsive and engaged team, focused on protecting what matters most to you.
7. **Be Happy, Healthy and Wealthy!**

Join our quest to live *Happily Ever Cyber!* at HappilyEverCyber.com

Glossary of Terms

Bits

It is the abbreviation of a binary digit and is the smallest unit of data in a computer, stores just 0 or 1.

Bytes

It is the term used to represent eight bits of data.

Bot

It is the abbreviation of Robot.

Cryptography

Refers to the study or practice of techniques to secure communications using codes, creating and solving them.

Cryptocurrency

It is a digital currency or asset that uses cryptography for security.

Cybersecurity

The techniques and practices to protect your computer, devices/tablets, phone, your network, data, software, and apps from cyber-attacks which are aiming to access, use, alter or delete your information, steal your identity or extort money from you.

Data Breach

Refers to a security incident that exposes information either intentionally or unintentionally.

Encryption

Refers to a process of encoding information in a way that only authorized people can read it.

Hackers

A skilled person who uses and exploits the weaknesses in computers or networks to gain unauthorized access to data for their personal gain.

Keylogger

It is a type of malware that records every keystroke as you type them, to gain access to your user-name and passwords or other confidential information.

Network

Is the group or collection of computers, systems or devices connected or linked to one another to allow the sharing of data or other resources.

Phishing

Fraudulent practice attempting to obtain sensitive information by sending emails pretending to be another company or a trustworthy entity inducing individuals to reveal their personal information.

Privacy

It is the right we have to control our information, how it is used, processed, stored, or shared.

Robocall

A telephone call placed to large numbers of people by a computerized device that automatically dials the telephone numbers and plays a recorded message.

Scam calls

Fraudulent phone calls to trick people to reveal personal information with the purpose of stealing your identity or money.

Spyware

It is a computer program or software designed to secretly monitor and gather information about how you use your computer.

Trojan horses

Also known as a Trojan horse, it is malware that misleads you to its true intent and hides in your computer and is usually designed to spy on, access, or extract your sensitive data.

Virus

It is a type of malware that infects your computer, programs, and files, and it spreads when executed, altering or stopping the way your computer operates.

Worm

It is a standalone malware program that copies itself to spread into other computers connected in the same network.

Bibliography and References

⟶ ❧ ⟵

Below are the resources and links used as references for the cybersecurity statistics in this book:

(1) Source: Gallup's Annual Crime Survey
https://news.gallup.com/poll/245336/one-four-americans-experienced-cybercrime.aspx

(2) Source: Cybersecurity Ventures
https://cybersecurityventures.com/cybersecurity-almanac-2019/

(3) Sources: Herjavec Group
https://www.herjavecgroup.com/wp-content/uploads/2018/12/CV-HG-2019-Official-Annual-Cybercrime-Report.pdf

(4) Source: Verizon Report 2019
https://enterprise.verizon.com/resources/reports/dbir/

(5) Source: Consumer Statistics
https://ipropertymanagement.com/research/iot-statistics
https://www.riskiq.com/infographic/evil-internet-minute-2019/
https://www.ftc.gov/sites/default/files/u269/csn-data-book-2018-infographic.png
https://robocallindex.com/history/time
https://selfkey.org/data-breaches-in-2019/
https://www.javelinstrategy.com/coverage-area/2018-child-identity-fraud-study
https://www.javelinstrategy.com/coverage-area/2018-child-identity-fraud-study

(6) Source: Symantec and Harris Poll 2018

https://www.symantec.com/content/dam/symantec/docs/about/2018-norton-lifelock-cyber-safety-insights-report-us-results-en.pdf

https://www.symantec.com/content/dam/symantec/docs/reports/istr-24-2019-en.pdf

Below are the sources used to research the layers of the ocean and the Internet specifically the deep and dark web. The ocean as well as the Internet is full of mysteries, and for now there is nothing that can fully reveal all the secrets that exist far, far, very far away.

(7) Ocean layers research

https://www.eartheclipse.com/geography/different-layers-of-the-ocean.html

https://timescavengers.blog/climate-change/ocean-layers-mixing/

https://www.worldatlas.com/articles/the-5-layers-of-the-ocean.html

https://sciencing.com/3-major-ocean-zones-22658.html

(8) Internet layers research

https://www.worldwidewebsize.com/

https://heimdalsecurity.com/blog/deep-web-vs-dark-web-what-is-each/

https://www.csoonline.com/article/3322134/10-things-you-should-know-about-dark-web-websites.html

https://www.recordedfuture.com/dark-web-reality/

https://resources.infosecinstitute.com/what-is-the-difference-between-the-surface-web-the-deep-web-and-the-dark-web/#gref

https://curiosity.com/topics/the-deep-web-is-the-99-of-the-internet-you-dont-see-curiosity/

https://digital.com/blog/deep-dark-web/

(9) Definitions inspired by https://dictionary.com

(10) Small business trends and statistics:

https://www.smallbizgenius.net/by-the-numbers/cyber-security-statistics/

(11) Cybersecurity talent shortages trends and statistics:

https://cybersecurityventures.com/research/

https://www.csis.org/analysis/cybersecurity-workforce-gap

https://www.mcafee.com/enterprise/en-us/assets/reports/rp-hacking-skills-shortage.pdf

(12) Orphans and Foster kids' research:

https://adoption.org/many-orphans-worldwide
https://www.covenanthouse.org/homeless-teen-issues/statistics
https://www.nfyi.
     org/51-useful-aging-out-of-foster-care-statistics-social-race-media/
https://adoption.com/how-many-orphans-in-the-us
https://www.nacac.org/2019/01/18/
     foster-care-numbers-up-for-fifth-straight-year/
https://www.childrensrights.org/newsroom/fact-sheets/foster-care/
Child Welfare Information Gateway. (2019). Foster care statistics 2017.
     Washington, DC: U.S. Department of Health and Human Services,
     Children's Bureau. https://www.childwelfare.gov/pubPDFs/foster.pdf
https://www.pewtrusts.org/en/research-and-analysis/blogs/
     stateline/2020/01/07/foster-care-adoptions-reach-record-high
https://www.childtrends.org/publications/supporting-older-
     youth-beyond-age-18-examining-data-and-trends-in-extended-foster-care
https://www.sos-usa.org/our-impact/focus-areas/advocacy-movement-
     building/childrens-statistics
https://www.unicef.org/media/media_45279.html
https://www.ifoster.org/6-quick-statistics-on-the-current-state-of-foster-care/
https://globalchildadvocates.org/socialorphans
https://www.storyintl.org/blog/2018/7/9/
     aging-out-what-happens-when-orphans-grow-up
https://en.wikipedia.org/wiki/Orphan

(13) All Fairy Tale quotes are from

https://www.goodreads.com/quotes/tag/fairy-tales with attribution to its
     authors.

(14) Website research

https://www.webarxsecurity.com/website-hacking-statistics-2018-february/
https://sucuri.net/reports/2019-hacked-website-report/

(15) Additional research related to identity theft and cybercrime

https://www.militaryonesource.mil/financial-legal/personal-finance/
     protecting-your-finances/keep-a-sharp-eye-out-for-identity-theft-and-scams
https://fraudsupport.org/incidents/extortion-scams/
https://www.econsumer.gov/#crnt
https://www.ic3.gov/complaint/default.aspx/
https://www.irs.gov/newsroom/tax-scams-consumer-alerts

https://staysafeonline.org/stay-safe-online/identity-theft-fraud-cybercrime/
reporting-cybercrime/
https://www.interpol.int/en/Crimes/Cybercrime

Additional Links and Information

The following websites and resources are available for you to consult regarding additional information about cybersecurity. They include the latest trends and advice to protect your families and businesses.

Basic guidelines for teens and parents about cyberbullying, sexting, social networking, and more: ConnectSafely.org

For parents, educators, and policymakers the information and tools which empower them to teach children the safe and healthy use of technology and the Internet: iKeepSafe.org

FTC's main consumer facing website to educate everyone on staying safe and secure online: OnGuardOnline.gov

Parent and Educator resources from Homeland Security: https://www.dhs.gov/publication/stopthinkconnect-parent-and-educator-resources

The National Cybersecurity Awareness Month (NCSAM) – resources available especially during October as it is Cyber Awareness month. https://staysafeonline.org/ncsam/

How to protect yourself against identity theft and respond if it happens: https://www.usa.gov/identity-theft

The FBI is the lead federal agency for investigating cyber-attacks: https://www.fbi.gov/investigate/cyber

Made in the USA
Monee, IL
18 June 2020

32989573R10095